# Wittgenstein *&* Religion

# Wittgenstein & Religion

*A Bibliography of Articles, Books, and Theses
in the Twentieth Century that Relate
the Philosophy of Ludwig Wittgenstein
to the Study of Religion and Theology*

Edited by DAVID STAGAMAN, S.J.
with JAMES KRAFT and KRISTIN SUTTON

OFFICE OF RESEARCH AND PUBLICATIONS
Ateneo de Manila University

Sources and Studies in the Critical Humanities
Budhi: A Journal of Ideas and Culture

General Editor

Luis S. David
Ateneo de Manila University

ISBN: 971-550-379-9

Cover Design: Oscar Bulaong, Jr.
With Assistance Provided by Nora Dela Cruz
    and Ana Maria Domingo

# Introduction

&

This bibliography was almost thirty years in the making. In the spring quarter of 1973, I offered a course for the Graduate Theological Union (GTU) entitled "Ordinary Language Philosophy." The students asked for a bibliography and one was produced, mostly on Wittgenstein and religion. Over the years the course has been offered at regular intervals, and the bibliography was regularly updated, eventually with the help of students in the course.

A few years ago I proposed to two GTU doctoral students, James Kraft and Kristin Sutton, that we prepare the present bibliography for publication. That proposal was occasioned by two facts: the closing of the twentieth century offered a convenient marker for inclusion and exclusion; the fiftieth anniversary of Wittgenstein's death in 2001 provided a certain timeliness for publication. James and Kristin agreed; and so we went to work.

The final version of the bibliography was a thoroughly collaborative undertaking. We met frequently in my faculty office, mapped out strategies for compiling the bibliography itself and its index, divided up the requisite tasks, and reported back to each other on progress.

James' computer skills proved invaluable. He and I together scanned available resources for entries. Along with Kristin, he developed the first version of the subject categories which I criticized as being too detailed. Gradually, the bibliography and the index took shape and were assembled on James' personal computer. He brought order out of what otherwise would have been chaos by entering the books, articles, and theses according to a consistent schema (the one available through the program Endnote), assigned the subject categories to various citations, and made sure that both the entries and the index appeared in readable English. In his disseration, Universal Truth Claims in Interreligious Dialogue, James will be making his own contribution to studies on Wittgenstein and religion, especially in Chapter Two where he uses "family resemblances" as a clue for forming a common ground for such dialogue.

James and Kristin also met separately themselves. Kristin made several contributions to the project. She helped to develop the subject headings and cross-referenced the entries in the bibliography to these headings. She was the principal proof-reader during the project. She also assisted James and myself in the research for bibliographic entries and compiled the final listing of these entries. Having completed this work, she is now beginning her doctoral dissertation at the GTU.

My own contribution was primarily the supervision of the overall project in light of my greater familiarity with the field. James and Kristin would remind me that it fell to yours truly to obtain funding for the project. This funding came from two sources: the Spohn faculty development fund at the Jesuit School of Theology at Berkeley; and financial grants from GTU which came through the kindness of Dean Margaret Miles. Both instutions and Dean Miles deserve out heartfelt gratitude.

The final editing of the bibliography and the index fell to yours truly. The numeration of the entries in the bibliography needed correction which entailed major revision in the index. I am especially grateful to Oscar Bulaong, Jr. and Nora dela Cruz of the Ateneo de Manila who assisted me in this effort.

My own interest in Wittgenstein goes back to my days as an M.A. student at Loyola University of Chicago where I first read the Philosophical Investigation. Ten years later in Paris I returned to Wittgenstein in my doctoral thesis which explored the use of Ordinary Language Philosophy in systematic theology.[1]

Over the years my interest in Wittgenstein has been kept alive, especially through participation in the Wittgenstein consultation of the American Academy of Religion and the Center for Hermeneutics in Berkeley. It has also been my pleasure to work with students in the M.A. and Ph.D. theses at the GTU (in the bibliography, see Caldwell, Ho, Rollefson, and Scobel). A forthcoming issue of BUDHI will contain my article, "Wittgenstein and the Religious Use of Language."

My own personal assessment, which is given in solid confidence, is that this bibliography is the most comprehensive available which links the philosophy of Ludwig Wittgenstein to the study of religion and theology. The subject index makes the various entries in the bibliography readily usable for students of Wittgenstein and religion. While most of the entries are in English, the attentive reader will recognize that we have scoured sources in several other languages for entries.

Final thanks for the publication of this work should go first to Luis David, S.J., for his encouragement. And James, Kristin, and I thank profoundly the Chicago Province of the Society of Jesus and its Provincial for granting the subsidy that the Ateneo de Manila Press needed for this publication.

David Stagaman, S.J.
Manila, March, 2001

[1]"'God' in Analytic Philosophy," GOD IN CONTEMPORARY THOUGHT, ed. Sebastian Matczak, New York: Learned Publications, 1977, pp. 813-849.

# BIBLIOGRAPHY

1   Abramson, Celene Charlotte. "Ethics in Wittgenstein." M.A. thesis, University of Virginia, 1987.

2   Aldwinckle, Russell Foster. "Much Ado About Words: Some Reflections on Language, Philosophy, and Theology." *Canadian Journal of Theology* 7 (1961): 91-98.

3   Alfaro, Juan. "Ludwig Wittgenstein ante la cuestión del sentido de la vida." *Gregorianum* 67 (1986): 693-744.

4   Allen, James Thomas. "Wittgenstein on Knowledge and Belief." M.A. thesis, Memphis State University, 1972.

5   Almeida, Ivan. "Discours inter-dit, discours transitionnel: reflexions métasémiotiques sur la nature du discours religieux." In *Theolinguistics*, ed. J. van Noppen, 47-62. Brussels: Vrije Universiteit Brussel, 1981.

6   Almond, Philip. "On the Varieties of Mystical Experience." *Sophia* 18 (1979): 1-9.

7   Almond, Philip. "Winch and Wittgenstein." *Religious Studies* 12 (1976): 473-482.

8   Almond, Philip. "Wittgenstein and Religion." *Sophia* 16 (1977): 24-27.

9   Alper, Harvey P. "The Cosmos as Siva's Language-game: 'Mantra' According to Ksemaraja's Sivasutravimarsini." In *Under-*

*standing Mantras*, ed. H. Alper, 249-294. Albany: State University of New York Press, 1989.

10   Altmann, Alexander. "The God of Religion, the God of Metaphysics and Wittgenstein's 'Language-games'." *Zeitschrift für Religions- und Geistesgeschichte* 39 (1987): 289-306.

11   Anderson, R. J., J. A. Hughes, and W. W. Sharrock. "Wittgenstein and Comparative Sociology." *Inquiry* 27 (1984): 268-276.

12   Anderson, Tyson. "Esotericism and the Essentialist Assumption." *Aries* (1990): 33-45.

13   Anderson, Tyson. "Wittgenstein and the Logical Possibility of Immortality." Ph.D. diss., Temple University, 1972.

14   Anscombe, G. E. M. "Wittgenstein." *World Review* January (1953): 3.

15   Antiseri, Dario. "Empirismo odierno e teologia nel caso 'Wittgenstein'." In *Filosofia e teologie contemporanee: atti del XXIX convegno del Centro di Studi Filosofici tra Professori Universitari Gallartin, '74*, ed. L. Sartori, 109-116. Brescia: Morcelliana, 1975.

16   Antiseri, Dario. "La 'mistica' di un 'logico': ovvero la religione in Ludwig Wittgenstein." *Proteus* 4 (1973): 163-170.

17   Apel, Karl Otto. "Wittgenstein und das Problem des hermeneutischen Verstehens." *Zeitschrift für Theologie und Kirche* 63 (1966): 49-87.

18   Arcenas, Bruno C. "The Signification of the Mystical in the *Tractatus Logico-philosophicus*." M.A. thesis, St. John's University, 1974.

19  Archer, Dermont J. "Küng, Wittgenstein and God." *Irish Theological Quarterly* 50 (1983-1984): 239-249.

20  Archer, Dermot J. "Tolstoy's God Sees the Truth, But Waits: A Reflection." *Religious Studies* 21 (1985): 75-89.

21  Ard, David John. "Language, Reality and Religion in the Philosophy of Ludwig Wittgenstein." Ph.D. diss., McMaster University, 1979.

22  Arens, Edmund. "Jesus' Communicative Actions: the Basis for Christian Faith Praxis, Witnessing, and Confessing." *Conrad Grebel Review* 3 (1985): 67-85.

23  Armengaud, Françoise. "Moore et Wittgenstein: 'Je crois que' - 'Je sais que'." In *On Believing: Epistemological and Semiotic Approaches*, ed. Herman Parret, 31-47. New York: W. de Gruyter, 1983.

24  Armour, Leslie, and Mostafa Faghfoury. "Wittgenstein's Philosophy and Religious Insight." *The Southern Journal of Philosophy* 22 (1984): 33-48.

25  Armstrong, Benjamin Franklin Jr. "Skepticism and Theories of Justification." Ph.D. diss., University of Pennsylvania, 1980.

26  Arnswald, Ulrich. "The Tension at the Core of the Tractatus." *Acta Analytica* (1998): 49-56.

27  Ayer, A. J. *Wittgenstein.* Chicago: University of Chicago Press, 1985.

28  Ayers, Robert H. "Language Theory and Analysis in Augustine." *Scottish Journal of Theology* 29 (1976): 1-12.

**29** Bahnsen, Greg L. "Philosophy: Pragmatism, Prejudice, and Presuppositionalism." In *Foundations of Christian Scholarship: Essays in the Van Til Perspective*, ed. Gary North, 241-292. Vallecito, California: Ross House Books, 1976.

**30** Baldini, Massimo. "Ludwig Wittgenstein (1889-1951): il silenzio, l'etica e la religione." In *Dio nella filosofia del Novecento*, ed. Giorgio Penzo, 247-255. Brescia: Queriniana, 1993.

**31** Balmuth, Jerome. "Wittgenstein and Religious Belief." In *Philosophy of Religion: International Wittgenstein Symposium 1983*, ed. W. Gombocz, 157-160. Vienna: Hölder-Pichler-Tempsky, 1984.

**32** Baltazar, Eulalio R. "Speaking of God in an Ever Changing World." In *Whither Creativity, Freedom, Suffering?: Humanity, Cosmos, God*, ed. Francis Eigo, 139-170. Villanova, Pa.: Villanova University Press, 1981.

**33** Bambrough, Renford. "Does Philosophy 'Leave Everything As It Is'? Even Theology?" *Philosophy* 25 (1989): 225-236.

**34** Bambrough, Renford. "Fools and Heretics." In *Wittgenstein Centenary Essays*, ed. A. Phillips Griffiths. New York: Cambridge University Press, 1991.

**35** Bambrough, Renford. *Reason, Truth and God.* London: Methuen, 1969.

**36** Banner, Michael C. "The Justification of Science and the Rationality of Religious Belief." Ph.D. diss., University of Oxford, 1986.

**37** Bar-Elli, Gilead. "Belief and Form of Life: Leibowitz and Wittgenstein [in Hebrew]." *Iyyun* 42 (1993): 493-508.

**38** Barrett, Cyril. *Etica y creencia religiosa en Wittgenstein.* Madrid: Alianza Editorial, 1994.

**39** Barrett, Cyril. "The Logic of Mysticism." In *Religion and Philosophy,* ed. Martin Warner, 61-69. Cambridge: Cambridge University Press, 1992.

**40** Barrett, Cyril. *Wittgenstein on Ethics and Religious Belief.* Cambridge, Mass.: Blackwell, 1991.

**41** Barrie, J. A. "The Autonomy of Religious Discourse." *Sophia* 19 (1980): 34-41.

**42** Bartley, W. "Wittgenstein and Homosexuality." In *Homosexuality and Religion and Philosophy,* ed. Wayne R. Dynes and Stephen Donaldson, 2-32. New York: Garland, 1992.

**43** Bassols, Alejandro Tomasini. "Conceptos religiosos y vida religiosa." *Dianoia* (1989): 91-105.

**44** Baum, Wilhelm. "Das Christentum als einzig sicherer Weg zum Glück. Neue Quellen zur negativen Theologie im *Tractatus.*" *Zeitschrift für Katholische Theologie* 104 (1982): 191-195.

**45** Baum, Wilhelm. "Ludwig Wittgenstein und die Religion." *Philosophisches Jahrbuch* 86 (1979): 272-299.

**46** Baum, Wilhelm. "Ludwig Wittgenstein's World View." *Ratio* 22 (1980): 64-74.

**47** Baum, Wilhelm. "Wittgensteins Tolstojanisches Christentum." *Conceptus* 11 (1977): 339-349.

**48** Baum, Wilhelm. "Wittgenstein's *Tractatus* as a 'Negative Theology' [in Czechoslovakian]." *Filozofia* 47 (1992): 212-220.

**49**   Beards, Andrew. "Anti-Realism and Criticial Realism: Dummett and Lonergan." *Downside Review* 113 (1995): 119-155.

**50**   Beardsley, Patrick J. "Aquinas and Wittgenstein on the Grounds of Certainty." *The Modern Schoolman* 51 (1974): 301-334.

**51**   Bearn, Gordon C. "Cavell, Wittgenstein, and Human Finitude." In *Philosophy of Religion: International Wittgenstein Symposium 1983*, ed. Wolfgang Gombocz, 95-97. Vienna: Hölder-Pichler-Tempsky, 1984.

**52**   Bearn, Gordon C. "Wittgenstein and the Uncanny." *Soundings* 76 (1993): 29-58.

**53**   Beckman, James. "Wittgenstein and Religious Belief." M.A. thesis, University of St. Michael's College, 1990.

**54**   Beehler, Rodger. *Moral Life.* Oxford: Blackwell, 1978.

**55**   Bejerholm, Lars. "Logiken i 'Guds ledning'." *Svensk Teologisk Kvartalskrift* 41 (1965): 25-38.

**56**   Bell, Richard H. "The Aesthetic Factor in Art and Religion." *Religious Studies* 22 (1986): 181-192.

**57**   Bell, Richard H. "Kierkegaard and Wittgenstein: Two Strategies for Understanding Theology." *The Iliff Review* 31 (1974): 21-34.

**58**   Bell, Richard H. "Religion and Wittgenstein's Legacy: Beyond Fideism and Language Games." In *Philosophy and the Grammar of Religious Belief*, ed. T. Tessin, 215-247. New York: St. Martin's Press, 1995.

59    Bell, Richard H. "Theology as Grammar: Is God an Object of Understanding?" *Religious Studies* 11 (1975): 307-317.

60    Bell, Richard H. "Theology as Grammar: Uses of Linguistic Philosophy for the Study of Theology with Special Reference to Ludwig Wittgenstein." Ph.D. diss., Yale University, 1968.

61    Bell, Richard H. "Understanding the Fire-Festivals: Wittgenstein and Theories in Religion." *Religious Studies* 14 (1978): 113-124.

62    Bell, Richard H. "Wittgenstein and Descriptive Theology." *Religious Studies* 5 (1969): 1-18.

63    Bell, Richard H., and Ronald E. Hustwit. *Essays on Kierkegaard & Wittgenstein: On Understanding the Self.* Wooster, Ohio: College of Wooster, 1978.

64    Berenson, Frances M. "Some Remarks About the Unutterable." *Philosophical Exchange: Annual Proceedings* 15-16 (1984): 61-76.

65    Bhat, P. R. "Wittgenstein and Svatahpramanyavada." In *East West Encounters in Philosophy and Religion,* ed. Ninian Smart. Long Beach: Long-Beach, 1996.

66    Bildhauer, William Mathias. "The Reality of God: An Investigation of the Adequacy of Wittgensteinian Fideism." Ph.D. diss., University of Arizona, 1972.

67    Bindeman, Steven Lee. "The Role of Silence in the Philosophies of Martin Heidegger and Ludwig Wittgenstein." Thesis, Duquesne University, 1978.

**68** Blackstone, William T. *The Problem of Religious Knowledge: The Impact of Philosophical Analysis on the Question of Religious Knowledge.* Englewood Cliffs NJ: Prentice-Hall, 1963.

**69** Bochenski, Joseph M. "Eröffnungsrede zum achten internationalen Wittgenstein-Symposium 1983." In *Philosophy of Religion: International Wittgenstein Symposium 1983,* ed. Gombocz Wolfgang, 21-34. Vienna: Hölder-Pichler-Tempsky, 1984.

**70** Boero, Mario. "Wittgenstein: Espiritualidad y mistica en su biografia." *Logos (Mexico)* 22 (1994): 39-81.

**71** Boero-Vargas, Mario. *Biografia y mistica de un pensador.* Madrid: Skolar, 1998.

**72** Bourbon, Brett Ryan. "Constructing a Replacement for the Soul: The Grammars of Self-Reflection and Temporality as the Limits of Language in *Finnegans Wake, Philosophical Investigations,* and Cognitive Science (Ludwig Wittgenstein, James Joyce, Martin Heidegger)." Ph.D. diss., Harvard University, 1996.

**73** Boutin, Maurice. "Méprises du langage, énigme du monde: à propos d'une expression étrange du Tractatus de Wittgenstein." *Religiologiques* (1990): 37-49.

**74** Bouveresse, Jacques. *Philosophie, mythologie et pseudo-science: Wittgenstein lecteur de Freud.* Combas, France: Editions de l'Eclat, 1991.

**75** Bouveresse, Jacques. "Wittgenstein on Frazer." In *A Wittgenstein Symposium,* ed. Josep-Maria Terricabras. Amsterdam: Rodopi, 1993.

76   Bouveresse, Jacques. *Wittgenstein, la rime et la raison. Science, éthique et esthétique.* Paris: Editions de Minuit, 1973.

77   Bouwsma, O. K. *Wittgenstein: Conversations 1949-1951.* Indianapolis: Hackett, 1986.

78   Braithwaite, R. B. *An Empiricist's View of the Nature of Religious Belief.* Cambridge: Cambridge University Press, 1955.

79   Bramann, John K. "Kafka and Wittgenstein on Religious Language." *Sophia (Australia)* 14 (1975): 1-9.

80   Bramann, John K. "Religious Language in Wittgenstein and Kafka." *Diogenes* 90 (1975): 26-35.

81   Brecher, Robert. "Karl Barth: Wittgensteinian Theologian Manqué." *Heythrop Journal* 24 (1983): 290-300.

82   Brenner, William H. "Chesterton, Wittgenstein and the Foundations of Ethics." *Philosophical Investigations* (1991): 311-323.

83   Brenner, William H. "Theology as Grammar." *The Southern Journal of Philosophy* 34 (1996): 439-454.

84   Brenner, William H. *Wittgenstein's Philosophical Investigations.* Albany: Suny, 1999.

85   Brent, Allen. "Transcendental Arguments for the Forms of Knowledge." *Journal of Philosophy of Education* 16 (1982): 265-274.

86   Bretall, Robert. "The Concept of Purpose in Reformation Thought." In *Religion and Human Purpose,* ed. W. Horosz and T. Clements, 165-195. Boston: M. Nijhoff, 1987.

**87** Breton, Stanislas. "Le sacré dans le langage philosophique." In *Prospettive sul sacro*, ed. E. Castelli, 15-26. Padova: CEDAM, 1975.

**88** Britton, Karl William. "Philosophische Ethik der Gegenwart in England; übersetzt von J Schollmeier." *Zeitschrift für Evangelische Ethik* 6 (1962): 101-115.

**89** Brose, Karl. "Religion und Ethik beim späten Wittgenstein: Zu Themen in Über Gewissheit." *Wittgenstein Studies* (1994).

**90** Browarzik, Ulrich. "Der grundlose Glaube: Wittgenstein über Religion." *Neue Zeitschrift für systematische Theologie und Religionsphilosophie* 30 (1988): 72-100.

**91** Brown, David. "Wittgenstein Against the 'Wittgensteinians': A Reply to Kenneth Surin on *The Divine Trinity*." *Modern Theology* 2 (1986): 257-276.

**92** Bruce, Graham A. "Wittgenstein, Relative Scientific, and Biblical Models and an Approach to Reality." *Theologia Evangelica* 21 (1988): 27-33.

**93** Bruening, William H. "Aquinas and Wittgenstein On God-Talk." *Sophia* 16 (1977): 1-7.

**94** Bruening, William H. "God Created Man." *Philosophical Studies (Ireland)* 29 (1982): 25-33.

**95** Bruening, William H. *Wittgenstein*. Washington DC: University Press of America, 1977.

**96** Brümmer, Vincent. "Has the Theism-Atheism Debate a Future?" *Theology* 97 (1994): 426-432.

**97**   Brümmer, Vincent. "Wittgenstein and the Irrationality of Rational Theology." In *The Christian Understanding of God Today: Theological Colloquium on the Occasion of the 400th Anniversary of the Foundation of Trinity College, Dublin*, ed. James Byrne, 88-102. Dublin: Columbia Press, 1993.

**98**   Brümmer, Vincent. "Wittgenstein en de natuurlijke theologie." *Nederlands Theologisch Tijdschrift* 48 (1994): 306-318.

**99**   Bugault, Guy. "Buddhist Anthropology vis-à-vis Modern Philosophy and Contemporary Neurophysiology." *Journal of Indian Council of Philosophical Research* (1990): 69-76.

**100**  Bugault, Guy. "L'anthropologie bouddhiste face à la philosophie moderne et à la neurophysiologie contemporaine." *Revue de l'Histoire des Religions* 203 (1986): 381-393.

**101**  Burghel, H. *Wittgenstein and His Impact on Contemporary Thought.* Vienna: Hölder-Pichler-Tempsky, 1978.

**102**  Burhenn, Herbert. "Religious Beliefs as Pictures." *Journal of the American Academy of Religion* 42 (1974): 326-335.

**103**  Burke, T. E. "The Justification of Belief." *Wittgenstein Studies* (1994).

**104**  Burke, T. E. "Theological Originality." *Religious Studies* 12 (1976): 1-20.

**105**  Burke, T. E. "Wittgenstein's *Lectures on Religious Belief*: A Reconsideration." In *Wittgenstein and His Impact*, ed. E. Leinfellner, 510-512. Vienna: Hölder-Pichler-Tempsky, 1978.

**106** Burkhardt, Armin. "Kant, Wittgenstein und das Verhältnis der relativen Ethik zur absoluten: zur Begründung einer Ökologischen Ethik." *Zeitschrift für Evangelische Ethik* 27 (1983): 391-431.

**107** Burnyeat, Myles F. "Wittgenstein and Augustine *De magistro.*" In *The Augustinian Tradition*, ed. Gareth B. Matthews, 286-303. Berkeley: University of California Press, 1999.

**108** Burr, Ronald. "Wittgenstein's Later Language-Philosophy and Some Issues in Philosophy of Mysticism." *International Journal for Philosophy of Religion* 7 (1976): 261-287.

**109** Burr, Ronald. "Wittgenstein's Non-Representational Religious Pictures." In *The Tasks of Contemporary Philosophy (Die Aufgaben der Philosophie in der Gegenwart)*, ed. Werner Leinfellner, 352-354. Vienna: Hölder-Pichler-Tempsky, 1986.

**110** Burrell, David B. "The Future of Philosophical Theology as Reflective Awareness." In *The Future of Philosophical Theology*, ed. Robert A. Evans, 85-112. Philadelphia: Westminster Press, 1970.

**111** Burrows, Mark S. "Naming the God Beyond Names: Wisdom from the Tradition on the Old Problem of God Language." *Modern Theology* 9 (1993): 37-53.

**112** Cady, Linell. "The Philosophical Passion of Ludwig Wittgenstein." In *Trajectories in Faith*, ed. Jim Fowler, 121-144. Nashville: Abingdon, 1980.

**113** Caine, Nadav. "Philosophical Prejudice and Religious Self-Understanding: Experience of 'The World' in Heschel, Buber, Wittgenstein, Davidson, and Rorty." *Koinonia* 5 (1993): 141-173.

**114** Caldwell, Christopher. "Wittgenstein's Public Theology." M.A. Thesis, Jesuit School of Theology at Berkeley/Graduate Theological Union, 1998.

**115** Cameron, J. M. "The Idea of Christendom." In *The Autonomy of Religious Belief*, ed. Frederick Crosson, 8-37. Notre Dame: Univiversity Notre Dame Press, 1981.

**116** Campana, Daniel A. "Faith and Knowledge." Ph.D. diss., The Claremont Graduate School, 1989.

**117** Campbell, James Ian. *The Language of Religion*. New York: Bruce, 1971.

**118** Canfield, John V., ed. *Aesthetics, Ethics and Religion*. New York: Garland, 1986.

**119** Canfield, John V. "Wittgenstein and Zen." *Philosophy* 50 (1975): 383-408.

**120** Canfield, John. V., and Stuart G. Shanker, eds. *Wittgenstein's Intentions*. New York: Garland, 1993.

**121** Caraboolad, Clemens Joseph. "Mysticism, Zen, and Wittgenstein." M.A. thesis, Kent State, 1976.

**122** Carlson, John W. "Investigations in the Grammar of Faith." *New Scholasticism* 57 (1983): 222-232.

**123** Carlson, John W. "Wittgenstein and Philosophy of Religion." In *History of Philosophy in the Making*, ed. Linus J. Thro. Washington: University Press of America, 1982.

**124** Carnap, R. "Intellectual Autobiography." In *The Philosophy of R. Carnap*, ed. P. Schilpp, 3-84. La Salle, Ill.: Open Court, 1963.

**125** Carse, James P. "Wittgenstein's Lion and Christology." *Theology Today* 24 (1967): 48-59.

**126** Casper, Bernhard. "Die Sprache und das Phänomen der Säkularisierung: Mythos oder Wirklichkeit, Verhängnis oder Verheissung?" In *Zum Problem der Säkularisierung*, ed. F. Theunis, 15-21. Hamburg-Bergstedt: H. Reich, 1977.

**127** Casper, Bernhard. "Die Unfähigkeit zur Gottesfrage im positivistischen Bewusstsein." In *Die Frage nach Gott*, ed. Joseph Ratzinger, 27-42. Freiburg: Herder, 1972.

**128** Casper, Bernhard. "Parole et le phénomène de la sécularisation." In *Herméneutique de la sécularisation*, ed. E. Castelli, 23-31. Paris: Aubier Montaigne, 1976.

**129** Cathey, Robert Andrew. "Foundations With Faces: A Prolegomenon to a Postliberal Doctrine of God." Ph.D. diss., Duke University, 1989.

**130** Cavell, Stanley. *The Cavell Reader*, ed. Stephen Mulhall. Cambridge: Blackwell, 1996.

**131** Cell, Edward. *Language, Existence and God: Interpretations of Moore, Russell, Ayer, Wittgenstein, Wisdom, Oxford philosophy, and Tillich*. New Jersey: Humanities Press, 1978.

**132** Chakrabarti, Arindam. "The End of Life: A Nyaya-Kantian Approach to the 'Bhagavadgita'." *Journal of Indian Philosophy* 16 (1988): 327-334.

**133** Chandra, Suresh. "Some Remarks on Wittgenstein on Religious Belief and Superstition." *Journal of Indian Council of Philosophical Research* 14 (1997): 153-164.

**134**   Chapman, Tobias. *In Defense of Mystical Ideas: Support for Mystical Beliefs from a Purely Theoretical Viewpoint.* Lewiston: Mellen Press, 1989.

**135**   Charlesworth, M. J. "Athéisme et philosophie analytique." In *Des Chretiens interrogent l'athéisme, 2/1*, ed. J. Six, 623-662. Paris: Desclee, 1970.

**136**   Charlesworth, M. J. "Linguistic Analysis and Language About God." *International Philosophical Quarterley* 1 (1961): 139-167.

**137**   Chatterjee, Ranjit. "Judaic Motifs in Wittgenstein." In *Austrians and Jews in the Twentieth Century*, ed. R. Wistrich, 142-161. New York: St. Martin's Press, 1992.

**138**   Chatterjee, Ranjit. "Wittgenstein as a Jewish Thinker." In *Proceedings of the 10th World Congress of Jewish Studies, Div C, v II: Jewish Thought and Literature*, ed. David Assaf. Jerusalem: World Union of Jewish Studies, 1990.

**139**   Cheng, Hsueh-Li. "Nagarjuna, Kant and Wittgenstein: The San-Lun Madhyamaka Exposition of Emptiness." *Religious Studies* 17 (1981): 67-85.

**140**   Cheng, Hsueh-Li. "Zen, Wittgenstein and Neo-Orthodox Theology: The Problem of Communicating Truth in Zen Buddhism." *Religious Studies* 18 (1982): 133-149.

**141**   Christian, Rose Ann. "Wittgenstein, Wittgensteinians and the Epistemological Status of Religious Belief." Ph.D. diss., University of Pennsylvania, 1981.

**142**   Churchill, John. "Beliefs, Principles, and Reasonable Doubts." *Religious Studies* 23 (1987): 221-232.

**143** Churchill, John. "Rat and Mole's Epiphany of Pan: Wittgenstein on Seeing Aspects and Religious Belief." *Philosophical Investigations* 21 (1998): 152-172.

**144** Churchill, John. "Something Deep and Sinister: Wittgenstein's Critique of J G Frazer on the Meaning of Ritual." *Modern Theology* 8 (1992): 15-37.

**145** Churchill, John. "The Squirrel Does Not Infer By Induction: Wittgenstein and the Natural History of Religion." In *Philosophy and the Grammar of Religious Belief,* ed. T. Tessin, 48-78. New York: St. Martin's Press, 1995.

**146** Churchill, John. "Walker Percy, Wittgenstein's *Tractatus,* and the Lost Self." *Soundings* 67 (1984): 267-282.

**147** Churchill, John. "Wittgenstein and Philosophy of Religion." Ph.D. diss., Yale University, 1977.

**148** Churchill, John. "Wittgenstein on Faith and Wisdom." *Southern Journal of Philosophy* 23 (1985): 413-430.

**149** Churchill, John. "Wittgenstein on the Phenomena of Belief." *International Journal for Philosophy of Religion* 16 (1984): 139-152.

**150** Churchill, John. "Wittgenstein's Adaptation of Schopenhauer." *Southern Journal of Philosphy* 21 (1983): 489-502.

**151** Churchill, John. "Wittgenstein's *Lectures on Religious Belief.*" *Sophia* 20 (1981): 33-39.

**152** Churchill, John. "Wonder and the End of Explanation: Wittgenstein and Religious Sensibility." *Philosophical Investigations* 17 (1994): 388-416.

**153** Churchill, Sandra Wade. "Thinking Through Language: Essays on Wittgenstein For Feminist Purposes." Ph.D. diss., The Union Institute, 1994.

**154** Churchland, John. "Beliefs, Principles, and Reasonable Doubts." *Religious Studies* 23 (1987): 221-232.

**155** Clack, Brian R. "D. Z. Phillips, Wittgenstein and Religion." *Religious Studies* 31 (1995): 111-120.

**156** Clack, Brian R. "Wittgenstein and Expressive Theories of Religion." *International Journal for Philosophy of Religion* 40 (1996): 47-61.

**157** Clark, Ralph W. "The Evidential Values of Religious Experience." *International Journal for Philosophy of Religion* 16 (1984): 189-202.

**158** Clarke, Bowman Lafayette. *Language and Natural Theology.* New York: Humanities Press, 1967.

**159** Clayton, John Powell. "Was ist falsch in der Korrelationstheologie?" *Neue Zeitschrift für systematische Theologie und Religionsphilosophie* 16 (1974): 93-111.

**160** Clegg, Jerry. "Faith." *American Philosophical Quarterly* 16 (1979): 225-232.

**161** Clegg, Jerry. *On Genius: Affirmation and Denial from Schopenhauer to Wittgenstein.* New York: Lang, 1994.

**162** Cleobury, Frank Harold. "Wittgenstein and the Philosophy of Religion." *The Modern Churchman* 13 (1970): 174-180.

**163** Coburn, Robert. "A Neglected Use of Theological Language." *Mind* 72 (1963): 369-385.

**164** Cockburn, David. "The Supernatural." *Religious Studies* 28 (1992): 285-301.

**165** Collins, Elizabeth Fuller. "A Ceremonial Animal." *Journal of Ritual Studies* 10 (1996): 59-84.

**166** Collopy, Bartholomew J. "Wittgenstein and Religious Discourse: Some Possibilities for *Theological Investigations*." Ph.D. diss., Yale University, 1972.

**167** Conant, James. "Putting Two and Two Together: Kierkegaard, Wittgenstein, and the Point of View for their Work as Authors." In *Philosophy and the Grammar of Religious Belief,* ed. T. Tessin, 248-331. New York: St. Martin's Press, 1995.

**168** Cook, John W. "Kierkegaard and Wittgenstein." *Religious Studies* 23 (1987): 199-219.

**169** Cook, John W. "Magic, Witchcraft and Science." *Philosophical Investigations* 6 (1983): 2-36.

**170** Cook, John W. "Religious Belief." In *Wittgenstein's Intentions,* ed. J. Canfield. Hamden: Garland, 1993.

**171** Cook, John W. "Wittgenstein and Religious Belief." *Philosophy* 63 (1988): 427-452.

**172** Cook, John W. *Wittgenstein's Metaphysics.* Cambridge: Cambridge University Press, 1994.

**173** Cooke, Vincent M. "Hans Küng on Propositions and Their Problematic: A Critique." *Thomist* 39 (1975): 753-765.

**174** Cooke, Vincent M. "Wittgenstein and Religion." *Thought* 61 (1986): 348-359.

175 Cooper, Neil. "The Religious Language Game." *Scottish Journal of Religious Studies* 9 (1988): 29-39.

176 Cordua, Carla. "La religiosidad de Wittgenstein." *Revista Agustiniana* 38 (1997): 789-825.

177 Coughlan, Michael J. "Wittgenstein, Language, and Religious Belief." In *God in Language*, ed. R. Scharlemann and G. Ogutu, 149-165. New York: Paragon House, 1987.

178 Coughlan, Michael J. "Wittgensteinian Philosophy and Religious Belief." *Metaphilosophy* 17 (1986): 230-240.

179 Coulson, John. "Catholics and the Revolution in Philosophy." *Downside Review* 76 (1958): 31-40.

180 Cox, Charles. "Wittgenstein's Concept of Language and Its Implications for Metaphysics and Theology." *Religious Humanism* 9 (1975): 79-83.

181 Cox, Charles. "Wittgenstein's Later Mysticism." *Religious Humanism* 13 (1979): 50-55.

182 Cox, Charles, and Jean Cox. "Mystical Experience: With an Emphasis on Wittgenstein and Zen." *Religious Studies* 12 (1976): 483-491.

183 Cox, Charles, and Jean Cox. "Wittgenstein: Religious Words and Humanistic Religion." *Religious Humanism* 14 (1980): 134-138.

184 Craft, J. L., and Ronald E. Hustwit, eds. *Without Proof or Evidence: Essays of O. K. Bouwsma*. Lincoln: University of Nebraska Press, 1984.

**185** Cranston, M. "L. Wittgenstein." *World Review* December (1951): 21-24.

**186** Creegan, Charles L. "Kierkegaard and Wittgenstein: A New Way of 'Doing Philosophy'." Ph.D. diss., Drew University, 1987.

**187** Creegan, Charles L. *Wittgenstein and Kierkegaard: Religion, Individuality, and Philosophical Method.* London: Routledge, 1989.

**188** Cripps, Peter. "A Note on Wittgenstein's Remark: 'Es ist schwer, mit einem Messer im Leib zu arbeiten'." In *Arbeiten zu Wittgenstein*, ed. H Wilhelm Kruger. Bergen: Wittgenstein Arch, 1998.

**189** Crosson, Frederick J., ed. *The Autonomy of Religious Belief: A Critical Inquiry.* Notre Dame: University of Notre Dame Press, 1981.

**190** Cruickshank, Andrew. "Wittgenstein and the Language of the Gospels." *Church Quarterly* 3 (1970): 40-51.

**191** Crunkleton, Martha Ann. "Wittgenstein and Philosophy of Religion." Ph.D. diss., Vanderbilt University, 1984.

**192** Curnutt, Jordan. "Huang on Wittgenstein on Religious Epistemology." *Religious Studies: An International Journal for the Philosophy of Religion* 34 (1998): 81-89.

**193** Curtis, Barry. "Wittgenstein and Ramakrishna on the Problem of Evil." In *East West Encounters in Philosophy and Religion*, ed. Ninian Smart. Long Beach: Long-Beach, 1996.

**194** Daly, C.B. "Logical Positivism, Metaphysics and Ethics." *Irish Theological Quarterly* 23 (1956): 111-150.

**195** Daly, C. B. "Miss Anscombe and 'Misinformation'." *Irish Theological Quarterly* 23 (1956): 147-150.

**196** Daly, C. B. "New Light on Wittgenstein." *Philosophical Studies (Ireland)* 10 (1961): 5-49.

**197** Daly, C.B. "Polanyi and Wittgenstein." In *Intellect and Hope*, ed. Thomas Langford and William Poteat. Durham: Duke University Press, 1968.

**198** Davie, I. A. N. *A Theology of Speech: An Essay in Philosophical Theology*. London: Sheed & Ward, 1973.

**199** Davies, Brian. "Scarlet O'Hara: A Portrait Restored." *Philosophy* 57 (1982): 402-407.

**200** Davies, Brian. "Speaking in Tongues: A Philosophical Comment." In *Strange Gifts?: A Guide to Charismatic Renewal*, ed. D. Martin and P. Mullen, 220-229. New York: Blackwell, 1984.

**201** Davies, Brian. "Wittgenstein on God." *Philosophy* 55 (1980): 105-108.

**202** Davies, Ivor. "Wittgenstein and the Bishop's Wife [Cecil Frances Alexander]." *The Modern Churchman* 23 (1980): 30-33.

**203** Davies, Philip. "Remarks on Wittgenstein's 'Remarks on Frazer's *The Golden Bough*'." *King's Theological Review* 6 (1983): 10-14.

**204** Davis, Grady Scott. "The Base of Design Relativism and Rationality in the Philosophy of Religion." Ph.D. diss., Princeton University, 1984.

205 D'Costa, Gavin. "Elephants, Ropes and a Christian Theology of Religions." *Theology* 88 (1985): 259-267.

206 DeAngelis, William James. "Ludwig Wittgenstein—A Religious Point of View? Thoughts on Norman Malcolm's Last Philosophical Project." *Dialogue: Canadian Philosophical Review* 36 (1997): 819-842.

207 DeAngelis, William M. "Wittgenstein and Spengler." *Dialogue (Canada)* 33 (1994): 41-61.

208 Della Santina, Peter. "The Madhyamaka and Modern Western Philosophy." *Philosophy East and West* 36 (1986): 41-54.

209 Devenish, Philip E. "The So-Called Resurrection of Jesus and Explicit Christian Faith: Wittgenstein's Philosophy, Marxsen's Exegesis as Linguistic Therapy." *Journal of the American Academy of Religion* 51 (1983): 171-190.

210 D'Hert, Ignace. *Wittgenstein's Relevance for Theology.* Bern: Peter Lange, 1978.

211 Diamond, Cora. "Riddles and Anselm's Riddle." *The Aristotelian Society: Supplementary Volume* 51 (1977): 143-168.

212 Diamond, Malcolm. "Review of Hudson's *Wittgenstein and Religious Belief.*" *Religious Studies* 15 (1979): 107-118.

213 Diamond, Malcolm. "Wisdom's Gods." *Sophia (Australia)* 22 (1983): 2-13.

214 Diamond, Malcolm. "Wittgenstein and Religion." *Religious Studies Review* 12 (1986): 17-22.

**215** Dilley, Frank B. "The Status of Religious Beliefs." *American Philosophical Quarterly* 13 (1976): 41-47.

**216** Dilman, Ilham. *Studies in Language and Reason.* Totowa, NJ: Barnes & Noble, 1981.

**217** Dilman, Ilham. "Wisdom's Philosophy of Religion—Part I: Religion and Reason." *Canadian Journal of Philosophy* 5 (1975): 473-495.

**218** Dilman, Ilham. "Wisdom's Philosophy of Religion—Part II: Metaphysical and Religious Transcendence." *Canadian Journal of Philosophy* 5 (1975): 497-521.

**219** Dipre, Gilio Louis. "The Language-Games of Wittgenstein: A Prolegomenon to a Metaphysics of Being." Ph.D. diss., St. Bonaventure University, 1968.

**220** Disbrey, Claire. *Innovation and Tradition in Religion: Towards an Institutional Theory.* Brookfield: Avebury, 1994.

**221** Donovan, John F. "Wittgenstein and Religious Language." Thesis (M.S.W.), St. Mary's Seminary (Baltimore, Md.), 1968.

**222** Dov Lerner, Berel. "Winch and Instrumental Pluralism." *Philosophy of the Social Sciences* 25 (1995): 180-191.

**223** Downey, John. *Beginning at the Beginning: Wittgenstein and Theological Conversation.* Lanham, MD: University Press of America, 1986.

**224** Downey, John. "Wittgenstein and the Foundations of Theology." Ph.D. diss., Marquette University, 1983.

225 Downing, F. Gerald. "Games, Families, the Public, and Religion." *Philosophy* 47 (1972): 38-54.

226 Dragona-Monachou, Myrto. "L. Wittgenstein's Ethical Aphorisms: The Modern 'to Himself' or How Can Silence Be Talked About." *Philosophia (Athens)* 10-11 (1980): 433-483.

227 Drewniak, Erik. "Two Postmodern Philosophies of God." *Dialogue (PST)* 36 (1993): 13-22.

228 Drob, Sanford L. "Judaism as a Form of Life." *Tradition* 23 (1988): 78-89.

229 Durrant, Michael. *The Logical Status of "God" and the Function of Theological Sentences.* London: Macmillan, 1973.

230 Durrant, Michael. "The Use of Pictures in Religious Belief." *Sophia (Australia)* 10 (1971): 16-21.

231 Eastmen, William O'Reilly. "Wittgenstein, Augustine and the Essence of Languages." *Philosophical Studies (Ireland)* 18 (1969): 110-118.

232 Edwards, James. "Deconstruction and the End of Philosophy: Kierkegaard, Wittgenstein, and the Hope of Salvation." In *Religion, Ontotheology and Deconstruction,* ed. H. Ruf, 183-210. New York: Paragon House, 1989.

233 Edwards, James. *Ethics Without Philosophy: Wittgenstein and the Moral Life.* Tampa: University Presses of Florida, 1982.

234 Edwards, James. *The Plain Sense of Things: The Fate of Religion in an Age of Normal Nihilism.* University Park: Pennsylvania State University Press, 1997.

**235**  Edwards, Rem B. *Reason and Religion, an Introduction to the Philosophy of Religion.* New York: Harcourt Brace Jovanovich, 1972.

**236**  Eisenstein, Gabe. "Understanding the Question: Wittgenstein on Faith and Meaning." *Religious Studies* 26 (1990): 463-470.

**237**  Eller, Vernard. *The Language of Canaan and the Grammar of Feminism.* Grand Rapids, Mich.: W.B. Eerdmans, 1982.

**238**  Elstein, Karen. "Wittgenstein's Early Ethics." M.A. thesis, University of Calgary (Canada), 1991.

**239**  Embree, Warren Charles. "Ethics and Interpretation (Hermeneutics, Paul, Augustine, Wittgenstein, Derrida)." Ph.D. diss., The University Of Nebraska - Lincoln, 1991.

**240**  Emmanuel, Steven M. "Kierkegaard on Doctrine: A Post-Modern Interpretation [Compared to G. A. Lindbeck]." *Religious Studies* 25 (1989): 363-378.

**241**  Engel, S. Morris. "Wittgenstein's Lectures and Conversations." *Dialogue* 7 (1969): 108-121.

**242**  Erben, David Lawrence. "Textual Space and Ritual Transformation in Contemporary Native American Fiction." Ph.D. diss., University of South Florida, 1997.

**243**  Erling, Bernhard. "Language Games and Contexts of Meaning: Wittgenstein and Anders Nygren." *Journal of the American Academy of Religion* 52 (1984): 691-708.

**244**  Ernst, Cornelius. "Words, Facts, and God (Problems Set by Wittgenstein for Metaphysical Theology)." *Blackfriars* 44 (1963): 292-306.

**245** Evans, Donald D. "Faith and Belief." *Religious Studies* 10 (1974): 1-19.

**246** Fahrenbach, Helmut. "Positionen und Probleme gegenwärtiger Philosophie." *Theologische Rundschau* 35 (1970): 277-306.

**247** Fahrenbach, Helmut. "Positionen und Probleme gegenwärtiger Philosophie." *Theologische Rundschau* 36 (1971): 125-144, 221-243.

**248** Fairley, James. "Method in Theology: Possibilities in the Light of Barth, Kierkegaard and Wittgenstein." Ph.D. diss., University of Aberdeen, 1991.

**249** Farrelly, John. "Religious Reflection and Man's Transcendence." *Thomist* 37 (1973): 1-68.

**250** Feinberg, John S. "Noncognitivism: Wittgenstein." In *Biblical Errancy: An Analysis of its Philosophical Roots*, ed. N. Geisler, 163-201. Grand Rapids: Zondervan Publishing House, 1978.

**251** Ferber, Rafael. "Der Grundgedanke des *Tractatus* als Metamorphose des obersten Grundsatzes der *Kritik der reinen Vernunft.*" *Freiburger Zeitschrift für Philosophie und Theologie* 33 (1986): 129-134.

**252** Ferré, Frederick. *Language, Logic and God.* New York: Harper, 1961.

**253** Ferreira, M. Jamie. "The Point Outside the World: Kierkegaard and Wittgenstein on Nonsense, Paradox and Religion." *Religious Studies* 30 (1994): 29-44.

254 Ferreira, M. Jamie. "Religion and 'Really Believing': Belief and the Real." In *Philosophy and the Grammar of Religious Belief,* ed. T. Tessin, 94-133. New York: St. Martin's Press, 1995.

255 Ferrelly, John. "Religious Reflection and Man's Transcendence." *The Thomist* 37 (1973): 1-68.

256 Festini, H. "Continuity of Wittgenstein's Views on Religious Belief (In Yugoslavian)." *Filozof Istraz* 28 (1989): 247-253.

257 Fiorenza, Francis Schüssler. "Theory and Practice: Theological Education as a Reconstructive, Hermeneutical, and Practical Task." *Theological Education* 23 (1987): 113-141.

258 Fitzpatrick, Joseph. "Philosophy of Religion: The Linguistic Approach." *Heythrop Journal* 19 (1978): 285-297.

259 Fleischacker, Samuel. "Religious Questions: Kafka and Wittgenstein on Giving Grounds." *Sophia* 21 (1982): 3-18.

260 Fleming, Jesse Charles. "Chuang Tsu and the Problem of Personal Identity: A Study of Identity and Interrelatedness." Ph.D. diss., University of Hawaii, 1988.

261 Fortuna, Joseph John. "Two Approaches to the Role of Language in Sacramental Efficacy Compared: Thomas Aquinas in the *Summa Theologiae* and Louis-Marie Chauvet." Thesis (S.T.D.), The Catholic University of America, 1989.

262 Foster, Patrick Milton. "The Paradigm of the Symbol: The Loss of 'Truth' in Twentieth-Century Thought." Ph.D. diss., University of California, Santa Barbara, 1995.

263 Frongia, Guido. "L. Wittgenstein: etica, estetica, psicoanalisi e religione." *Giornale Critico della Filosofia Italiana* 50 (1971): 120-130.

264 Funk, Warren Howard. "Religion, Belief, and the Expression of Belief: Toward a Philosophical Characterization of Religious Belief with Special Reference to Ludwig Wittgenstein." Ph.D. diss., Columbia University, 1981.

265 Gaita, Raimond. *Value and Understanding: Essays for Peter Winch.* New York: Routledge, 1990.

266 Gallagher, M.P. "Wittgenstein's Admiration for Kierkegaard." *The Month* 39 (1968): 43-49.

267 Garceau, B. "La Philosophie analytique de la religion: contribution canadienne." *Philosophiques* 2 (1975): 301-339.

268 Garner, Dick. "Skepticism, Ordinary Language and Zen Buddhism." *Philosophy East and West* 27 (1977): 165-181.

269 Garner, Richard T. "The Deconstruction of the Mirror and Other Heresies: Ch'an and Taoism as Abnormal Discourse." *Journal of Chinese Philosophy* 12 (1985): 155-168.

270 Garver, Newton. "Pantheism and Ontology in Wittgenstein's Early Work." *Idealistic Studies: An Interdisciplinary Journal of Philosophy* 1 (1971): 269-277.

271 Gasking, D. A. T., and A. C. Jackson. "Ludwig Wittgenstein." *Australasian Journal of Philosophy* 29 (1951): 73-83.

272 Gastwirth, Paul. "Concepts of God." *Religious Studies* 10 (1974): 147-152.

**273**  Gastwirth, Paul. "Reply to Peter Slater." *Religious Studies* 10 (1974): 85-88.

**274**  Gay, Volney P. "Reductionism and Redundancy in the Analysis of Religious Forms." *Zygon* 13 (1978): 169-183.

**275**  Gehl, Paul F. "An Answering Silence: Claims for the Unity of Truth Beyond Language." *Philosophy Today* 30 (1986): 224-233.

**276**  Geisler, Norman. "Philosophy: Roots of Vain Deceit." *Christianity Today* 21 (1977): 8-12.

**277**  Geisler, Norman L. ed. *Biblical Errancy: An Analysis of its Philosophical Roots.* Grand Rapids: Zondervan, 1978.

**278**  Genova, Judith. "An Approach to Wittgenstein's Metaphysics." Thesis, Brandeis University, 1970.

**279**  Geuras, Dean. "Orthodoxy and Contemporary Linguistic Philosophy in Historical Perspective." *Patristic and Byzantine Review* 3 (1984): 223-232.

**280**  Gill, Jerry. "God-talk: Getting On With It. A Review of Current Literature." *Southern Journal of Philosophy* 6 (1968): 115-124.

**281**  Gill, Jerry. "Mediated Meaning: A Contextualist Approach to Hermeneutical Method." *Asbury Theological Journal* 43 (1988): 27-41.

**282**  Gill, Jerry. *On Knowing God.* Philadelphia: Westminster, 1981.

**283**  Gill, Jerry. "Posing as an Artist as an Old Man: An Interdisciplinary Encounter." *Christian Scholar's Review* 8 (1978): 46-51.

**284** Gill, Jerry. *The Possibility of Religious Knowledge.* Grand Rapids: Eerdmans, 1971.

**285** Gill, Jerry. "Post-Critical Philosophy of Religion." *International Philosophical Quarterly* 22 (1982): 75-86.

**286** Gill, Jerry. "Religious Experience as Mediated." *Christian Scholar's Review* 13 (1984): 349-359.

**287** Gill, Jerry. "Saying and Showing: Radical Themes in Wittgenstein's *On Certainty.*" *Religious Studies* 10 (1974): 279-290.

**288** Gill, Jerry. "Shaping and Being Shaped." *Christian Century* 92 (1975): 685-688.

**289** Gill, Jerry. "Tacit Knowing and Religious Belief." *International Journal for Philosophy of Religion* 6 (1975): 73-88.

**290** Gill, Jerry. "The Tacit Structure of Religious Knowing." *International Philosophical Quarterly* 9 (1969): 533-559.

**291** Gill, Jerry. "What Wittgenstein Wasn't: Critique of Contemporary Interpreters." *International Philosophical Quarterly* 30 (1990): 207-220.

**292** Gill, Jerry. "Winch, Science, and Embodiment." *Soundings* 65 (1982): 417-429.

**293** Gill, Jerry. "Wittgenstein and Religious Language." *Theology Today* 21 (1964-1965): 59-72.

**294** Gillett, Grant R. "Brain, Mind, and Soul." *Zygon* 20 (1985): 425-434.

**295** Glebe-Moller, Jens. "Marx and Wittgenstein on Religion and the Study of Religion." In *Wittgenstein and His Impact on Contemporary Thought*, ed. E. Leinfellner, 525-528. Vienna: Hölder-Pichler-Tempsky, 1978.

**296** Glebe-Moller, Jens. "Two Views of Religion in Wittgenstein." In *The Grammar of the Heart: New Essays in Moral Philosophy and Theology*, ed. Richard H. Bell. San Francisco: Harper and Row, 1988.

**297** Glebe-Moller, Jens. "Wittgenstein and Kierkegaard." In *Kierkegaardiana (15)*, ed. J. Garff, 55-68. Copenhagen: Reitzels Forlag, 1991.

**298** Glebe-Moller, Jens. *Wittgenstein og religionen*. Kobenhavn: Gad, 1969.

**299** Glidden, David K. "Josiah Royce's Reading of Plato's 'Theaetetus'." *History of Philosophy Quarterly* 13 (1996): 273-286.

**300** Goff, Robert. "Language of Method in Wittgenstein's *Philosophical Investigations*." *Drew Gateway* 40 (1970): 149-150.

**301** Goff, Robert Allen. "The Wittgenstein Game." *Christian Scholar* 45 (1962): 179-197.

**302** Goodman, R. "How a Thing is Said and Heard: Wittgenstein and Kierkegaard." *History of Philosophy Quarterly* 3 (1986): 335-353.

**303** Goodman, Russell. "Style, Dialectic, and the Aim of Philosophy in Wittgenstein and the Taoists." *Journal of Chinese Philosophy* 3 (1976): 145-158.

**304** Grabner-Haider, A. "Wittgenstein und 'das Mystische'. Folgerungen für die Theologie." *Zeitschrift für Philosophische Forschung* 97 (1975): 282-296.

**305** Graf, Georg. "Am Grunde des begründeten Glaubens liegt der unbegündete Glaube: Wittgenstein über Religion und Wissenschaft." In *Philosophy of Religion: International Wittgenstein Symposium 1983*, ed. W. Gombocz, 230-232. Vienna: Hölder-Pichler-Tempsky, 1984.

**306** Grafrath, Bernd. "Wissenschaftstheorie oder Ästhetik der Wunder?" *Theologie und Philosophie: Vierteljahresschrift* 72 (1997): 257-263.

**307** Graham, G. "Mystery and Mumbo-Jumbo." *Philosophical Investigations* 7 (1984): 281-294.

**308** Grant, Brian. "Wittgenstein's Elephant and Closet Tortoise." *Philosophy* 70 (1995): 191-215.

**309** Grassi, Ernesto. "Terreur de la sécularisation: la métaphore vide." In *Herméneutique de la sécularisation*, ed. E. Castelli, 33-48. Paris: Aubier Montaigne, 1976.

**310** Greisch, Jean. "La religion à l'intérieur des limites du simple langage." In *Penser la religion: recherches en philosophie de la religion*, ed. J. Greisch, 321-380. Paris: Beauchesne, 1991.

**311** Grennan, Wayne. "Wittgenstein on Religious Utterances." *Sophia (Australia)* 15 (1976): 13-18.

**312** Griffiths, A. Phillips, ed. *Wittgenstein Centenary Essays*. New York: Cambridge University Press, 1991.

313 Grillo, Andrea. "Per una genealogia della libertà: il 'mistico' nel secondo Wittgenstein e il ruolo della teologia in una filosofia della mistica." In *Filosofia e mistica*, ed. Aniceto Molinaro and Elmar Salmann, 89-127. Rome: Pont Ateneo S Anselmo, 1997.

314 Grim, Patrick. "Logic and Limits of Knowledge and Truth." *Nous* 22 (1988): 341-367.

315 Gruenler, Royce G. "Implied Christological Claims in the Core Sayings of Jesus: An Application of Wittgenstein's Phenomenology." *Society of Biblical Literature: Seminar Papers* (1981): 65-77.

316 Grünfeld, Joseph. "Laudan's Research Tradition." *Science et Esprit* 35 (1983): 117-125.

317 Grünfeld, Joseph. "Raising the Ghost in the Machine." *Science et Esprit* 27 (1975): 91-105.

318 Guarino, Thomas. "'Spoils from Egypt': Contemporary Theology and Non-Foundationalist Thought." *Laval Théologique et Philosophique* 51 (1995): 573-587.

319 Gudmunsen, Chris. "On the Mahayana and Wittgenstein." *Religion* 4 (1974): 96-103.

320 Gudmunsen, Chris. *Wittgenstein and Buddhism*. London: Macmillan, 1977.

321 Gurrey, C. S. "Faith and the Possibility of Private Meaning: A Sense of the Ineffable in Kierkegaard and Murdoch." *Religious Studies* 26 (1990): 199-205.

**322**  Guth, Hermann. *The Amish-Mennonites of Waldeck and Wittgenstein.* Elverson, PA: Mennonite Family History, 1986.

**323**  Gutting, Gary. *Religious Belief and Religious Skepticism.* Notre Dame: University of Notre Dame Press, 1982.

**324**  Habermas, Jürgen. "A Review of Gadamer's *Truth and Method.*" In *Hermeneutics and Modern Philosophy,* ed. B. Wachterhauser, 243-276. Albany, New York: State University of New York Press, 1986.

**325**  Haden, N. Karl. "Sufferings of Inwardness: An Analysis of Religious Belief and Existence in the Thought of Kierkegaard and Wittgenstein." Ph.D. diss., University of Georgia, 1991.

**326**  Haikola, Lars. "Att tro och icke-tro i språkspelsteorin." In *Iustificatio impii: jumalattoman vanhurskauttaminen: juhlakirja professori Lauri Haikolan tayttaessa 60 vuotta 9. 2. 1977,* ed. J. Talasniemi, 66-72. Helsinki: Suomalainen Teologinen Kirjallisuusseural, 1977.

**327**  Haikola, L. *Religion as Language Game. A Critical Study with Special Regard to D. Z. Phillips.* Lund: Gleerup, 1976.

**328**  Hall, Elton Arthur. "A Proposed Application of the Principles of Wittgenstein to the Methodology of Tillich." Thesis, Occidental College, 1963.

**329**  Hall, Thor. "Wittgensteinian Fideism or Analytical Orderliness in Nygren's *Meaning and Method?*" *Perspectives in Religious Studies* 6 (1979): 66-75.

**330**  Haller, Rudolf. "Bemerkungen zur Egologie Wittgensteins." In *Wittgenstein in Focus—Im Brennpunkt: Wittgenstein,* ed. Brian McGuinness and Rudolf Haller. Amsterdam: Rodopi, 1989.

**331** Hallett, Garth L. *Darkness and Light: The Analysis of Doctrinal Statements.* New York: Paulist Press, 1975.

**332** Hallett, Garth L. "The Genesis of Wittgenstein's Later Philosophy in His Failure as a Phenomenologist." *Philosophy and Theology* 5 (1991): 297-312.

**333** Hallett, Garth L. "Light Dawns Gradually Over the Whole." *Heythrop Journal* 18 (1977): 316-319.

**334** Hallett, Garth L. "Theoretical Content of Language." *Gregorianum* 54 (1973): 307-337.

**335** Hallett, Garth L. "Wittgenstein and the 'Contrast Theory of Meaning'." *Gregorianum* 51 (1970): 679-710.

**336** Hamilton, James R. "What If There Were a Religious 'Form of Life'?" *Philosophical Investigations* 2 (1979): 1-17.

**337** Hampe, Michael. "Gesetz, Befehle und Theorien der Kausalitat." *Neue Hefte für Philosophie* 32-33 (1992): 15-49.

**338** Hannay, Alastair. *Kierkegaard.* London, Boston: Routledge and K. Paul, 1982.

**339** Hannay, Alastair. "Solitary Souls and Infinite Help: Kierkegaard and Wittgenstein." *History of European Ideas* 12 (1990): 41-52.

**340** Hargrove, Eugene C. "Moria: A Computer Simulation for Introductory Philosophy." *Teaching Philosophy* 9 (1986): 219-236.

**341** Harrison, Frank. "Talk about God: Can God-Language Be Meaningful, Wittgenstein and Ayer." *Iliff Review* 21 (1964): 49-54.

**342** Harrison, Frank. "To the Skeptic: A Wittgensteinian Response." *Dialogue and Alliance* 1 (1988): 45-55.

**343** Hartnack, Justus. "Analytic Philosophy and the Research on the Conceptualizations of an Ultimate Reality and Meaning of Human Existence." *Ultimate Reality and Meaning* 4 (1981): 151-162.

**344** Harvey, Michael G. "Wittgenstein's Notion of 'Theology as Grammar'." *Religious Studies* 25 (1989): 89-103.

**345** Harvey, Van Austin. "The Alienated Theologian." In *The Future of Philosophical Theology*, ed. R. Evans, 113-143. Philadelphia: Westminster Press, 1971.

**346** Hawkins, Denis John Bernard. *Wittgenstein and the Cult of Language: A Paper Read to the Aquinas Society of London in 1956.* Aquinas Society of London, no. 27. London: Blackfriars, 1957.

**347** Hayes, John. "Wittgenstein, Religion, Freud, and Ireland." *Irish Philosophical Journal* 6 (1989): 191-249.

**348** Heaney, James. "Faith and the Logic of Seeing-As." *International Journal for Philosophy of Religion* 10 (1979): 189-198.

**349** Heaney, James. "The Logic of Questions and the Existence of God." *Religious Studies* 16 (1980): 203-216.

**350** Heimbeck, Raeburne Seeley. *Theology and Meaning: A Critique of Metatheological Scepticism.* Stanford: Stanford University Press, 1969.

**351** Hellerer, Heinz. "Tolstois Kurze Auslegung des Evangeliums und Wittgensteins Tractatus Logico-Philosophicus." In *Philosophy of Religion: International Wittgenstein Symposium 1983*, ed. W. Gombocz, 164-166. Vienna: Hölder-Pichler-Tempsky, 1984.

**352** Helme, Mark. "Barth and Philosophy." *Heythrop Journal* 22 (1981): 285-289.

**353** Henderson, Edward Hugh. "Austin Farrer and D. Z. Phillips on Lived Faith, Prayer and Divine Reality." *Modern Theology* 1 (1985): 223-243.

**354** Henderson, Edward H. "Theistic Reductionism and the Practice of Worship." *International Journal for Philosophy of Religion* 9 (1979): 25-40.

**355** Henry, Granville. *Logos: Mathematics and Christian Theology.* Lewisburg: Bucknell, 1976.

**356** Henry, Granville C., Jr. "Mathematics, Phenomenology, and Language Analysis in Contemporary Theology." *Journal of the American Academy of Religion* 35 (1967): 337-349.

**357** Henze, Donald F. "Language Games and the Ontological Argument." *Religious Studies* 4 (1968): 147-152.

**358** Herbert, R. T. *Paradox and Identity in Theology.* Ithaca: Cornell, 1979.

**359** Herrmann, Eberhard. "The Rationality of Ideologies and Religions." *Nederlands Theologisch Tijdschrift* 45 (1991): 223-238.

**360** Hess, Gérald. "Le Tractatus de Wittgenstein: considérations sur le système numérique et la forme aphoristique." *Revue de Théologie et de Philosophie* 121 (1989): 389-406.

**361** Hesse, Mary. "Talk of God." *Philosophy* 44 (1969): 343-349.

**362** High, Dallas. "Belief, Falsification, and Wittgenstein." *International Journal for Philosophy of Religion* 3 (1972): 240-250.

**363** High, Dallas. *Language, Persons, and Belief: Studies in Wittgenstein's Philosophical Investigations and Religious Uses of Language.* New York: Oxford University Press, 1967.

**364** High, Dallas, ed. *New Essays on Religious Language.* New York: Oxford University Press, 1969.

**365** High, Dallas. "On Thinking More Crazily than Philosophers: Wittgenstein, Knowledge and Religious Beliefs." *International Journal for Philosophy of Religion* 19 (1986): 161-175.

**366** High, Dallas. "Wittgenstein on Doubting and Groundless Believing." *Journal of the American Academy of Religion* 49 (1981): 249-266.

**367** High, Dallas. "Wittgenstein: On Seeing Problems from a Religious Point of View (Presidential Address to Society for the Philosophy of Religion, 1989)." *International Journal for Philosophy of Religion* 28 (1990): 105-117.

**368** Hill, Roscoe Earl. "The Future of Ontotheology." In *Religion, Ontotheology and Deconstruction,* ed. H. Ruf, 211-226. New York: Paragon House, 1989.

**369** Hill, William J. "On 'Knowing the Unknowable God': A Review Discussion." *Thomist* 51 (1987): 699-709.

**370** Ho, Marjorie Jones. "Wittgenstein and Religious Certainty." M.A. Thesis, Jesuit School of Theology at Berkeley/Graduate Theological Union, 1991.

**371** Hodges, Michael P. "Faith—Themes in Wittgenstein and Kierkegaard." In *Philosophy and Culture, V3: Proceedings of the XVII World Congress of Philosophy*, ed. Venant Cauchy. Montreal: Editions Montmorency, 1988.

**372** Hoffman, Robert. "Logic, Meaning, and Mystical Intuition." *Philosophical Studies: An International Journal for Philosophy in the Analytic Tradition* 11 (1960): 65-70.

**373** Hofmeister, Heimo. "Wittgensteins Sprachspiele und ihre Bedeutung für die analytische Religionsphilosophie." In *Wittgenstein and His Impact on Contemporary Thought: Proceedings of the Second International Wittgenstein Symposium*, ed. E. Leinfellner, 517-520. Vienna: Hölder-Pichler-Tempsky, 1978.

**374** Holland, R. F. "Not Bending the Knee: Philosophical Religion and Historical Religion." *Philosophical Investigations* 13 (1990): 18-30.

**375** Holmer, Paul. "About Religious Consciousness." *Lutheran Quarterly* 23 (1971): 138-149.

**376** Holmer, Paul. *The Grammar of Faith*. San Fransisco: Harper and Row, 1978.

**377** Holmer, Paul. "Indirect Communication: Something about the Sermon (with References to Kierkegaard and Wittgenstein)." *Perkins Journal* 24 (1971): 14-24.

378  Holmer, Paul. "Post-Kierkegaard: Remarks about Being a Person." In *Kierkegaard's Truth*, ed. J. Smith, 3-22. New Haven: Yale University Press, 1981.

379  Holmer, Paul. "Wittgenstein and Theology." In *New Essays on Religious Language*, ed. Dallas High. New York: Oxford University Press, 1969.

380  Holmer, Paul. "Wittgenstein: 'Saying' and 'Showing'." *Neue Zeitschrift für systematische Theologie und Religionsphilosophie* 22 (1980): 222-235.

381  Holmes, Arthur F. *Christian Philosophy in the 20th Century: An Essay in Philosophical Methodology*. Nutley NJ: Craig Press, 1969.

382  Hopkins, Jasper. "On Understanding and Preunderstanding St. Anselm." *New Scholasticism* 52 (1978): 243-260.

383  Horne, James R. "How to Describe Mystical Experiences." *Studies in Religion/Sciences religieuses* 6 (1976): 279-84.

384  Huang, Yong. "Religious Beliefs after Foundationalism: Wittgenstein between Nielsen and Phillips." *Religious Studies: An International Journal for the Philosophy of Religion* 31 (1995): 251-267.

385  Hubík, Stanislav. "Wittgenstein, Religion, Atheism." In *Philosophy of Religion: International Wittgenstein Symposium 1983*, ed. W. Gombocz, 173-176. Vienna: Hölder-Pichler-Tempsky, 1984.

386  Hudson, William Donald. "The Concept of Divine Transcendence." *Religious Studies* 15 (1979): 197-210.

**387** Hudson, William Donald. "The Light Wittgenstein Sheds on Religion." *Midwest Studies in Philosophy* 6 (1981): 275-292.

**388** Hudson, William Donald. *Ludwig Wittgenstein.* London: Lutterworth, 1968.

**389** Hudson, William Donald. *Ludwig Wittgenstein: The Bearing of his Philosophy upon Religious Belief.* Makers of Contemporary Theology. Richmond: John Knox Press, 1970.

**390** Hudson, William Donald. "On Two Points Against Wittgensteinian Fideism." *Philosophy* 43 (1968): 269-273.

**391** Hudson, William Donald. *A Philosophical Approach to Religion.* London: Macmillan, 1974.

**392** Hudson, William Donald. "Some Remarks on Wittgenstein's Account of Religious Belief." In *Talk of God,* 36-51. New York: Macmillan, 1969.

**393** Hudson, William Donald. "The Two Factors in Religious Experience." In *Vardag och Evighet,* ed. B. Hanson, 141-146. Lund: Doxa, 1981.

**394** Hudson, William Donald. "'Using a Picture' and Religious Belief." *Sophia* 12 (1973): 11-17.

**395** Hudson, William Donald. "What Makes Religious Beliefs Religious?" *Religious Studies* 13 (1977): 221-242.

**396** Hudson, William Donald. *Wittgenstein and Religious Belief.* London: Macmillan, 1975.

**397** Hudson, William Donald. "Wittgenstein and Zen Buddhism." *Philosophy East and West* 23 (1973): 471-481.

**398** Hudson, William Donald. *Wittgensteinian Fideism.* New York: Doubleday, 1970.

**399** Huff, Douglas. "Wittgenstein, Solipsism, and Religious Belief." *Sophia (Australia)* 31 (1992): 37-52.

**400** Hughes, M. W. "Aspectual and Religious Perceptions." *Sophia* 7 (1968): 3-11.

**401** Hull, Kathleen. "Why Hanker After Logic? Mathematical Imagination, Creativity and Perception in Peirce's Systematic Philosophy." *Transactions of the Charles S. Peirce Society: A Quarterly Journal in American Philosophy* 30 (1994): 271-296.

**402** Hurley, S. L. "Objectivity and Disagreement." In *Morality and Objectivity*, ed. T. Honderich, 54-97. Boston: Routledge and Kegan Paul, 1985.

**403** Hurley, S. L. *Wittgenstein on Practice and the Myth of Giving.* Lindley Lecture. Lawrence: Department of Philosophy, University of Kansas, 1995.

**404** Hustwit, Ronald. "Adler and the Ethical: A Study of Kierkegaard's *On Authority and Revelation.*" *Religious Studies* 21 (1985): 331-348.

**405** Hustwit, Ronald. "More Notes on Kierkegaard's 'Ideal Interpretation'." *Journal of Religious Studies (Ohio)* 8 (1980): 12-18.

**406** Hustwit, Ronald. *Something About O. K. Bouwsma.* Lanham, MD: University Press of America, 1992.

**407** Hustwit, Ronald. "Understanding a Suggestion of Professor Cavell's: Kierkegaard's Religious Stage as a Wittgensteinian 'Form of Life'." *Philosophy Research Archives* 4 (1978).

**408** Inbody, Tyron ed. "The Relevance of William James for Philosophy and Theology in the 1990s." *American Journal of Theology and Philosophy* 15 (1994): 3-85.

**409** Incandela, Joseph M. "The Appropriation of Wittgenstein's Work by Philosophers of Religion: Towards a Re-evaluation and an End." *Religious Studies* 21 (1985): 457-474.

**410** Inciarte, Fernando. "El problema de la verdad en la filosofía actual y en Santo Tomás." In *Veritas et sapientia*, ed. J. Rodriguez Rosado, 41-59. Pamplona: Ediciones Universidad de Navarra, 1975.

**411** Indiana, Gary. "Ludwig Wittgenstein, Architect." *Art in America* 73 (1985): 112-133.

**412** Insole, Christopher. "A Wittgensteinian Philosophy of Religion—Or a Philosophy of Wittgensteinian Religion?" *Heythrop Journal: A Quarterly Review of Philosophy and Theology* 39 (1998): 148-157.

**413** Irwin, Alec. "Face of Mystery, Mystery of a Face: An Anthropological Trajectory in Wittgenstein, Cavell, and Kaufman's Biohistorical Theology." *Harvard Theological Review* 88 (1995): 389-409.

**414** Jacquette, Dale. *Meinongian Logic: The Semantics of Existence and Nonexistence.* Hawthorne: de Gruyter, 1996.

**415** Jager, Ronald. *The Development of Bertrand Russell's Philosophy.* New York: Humanities Press, 1972.

**416** Jarrett, Michael Stevens. "Sketches of Change in the Thinking of L. Wittgenstein with Implications for Religious Belief." M.A. thesis, Vanderbilt University, 1994.

**417** Jasper, David. "The New Testament and Literary Interpretation." *Religion and Literature* 17 (1985): 1-10.

**418** Jespers, Frans P.M. "Reflections on the Declaration of a Global Ethic." *Studies in Interreligious Dialogue* 8 (1998): 60-73.

**419** John, Peter. "A Sense of Wonder: Reassessing the Life and Work of Ludwig Wittgenstein." Ph.D. diss., University of California, San Diego, 1988.

**420** John, Peter. "Wittgenstein's 'Wonderful Life'." *Journal of the History of Ideas* 49 (1988): 495-510.

**421** Johnson, Charles W. "An Oath of Silence: Wittgenstein's Philosophy of Religion." *Philosophy and Theology* 5 (1991): 283-295.

**422** Johnson, Ralph H. "Wittgenstein: Philosophy and Grammar." In *Philosophy and Christian Theology*, ed. G. McLean and J. Dougherty, 99-107. Washington, D.C.: The Catholic University of America, 1970.

**423** Johnston, Scott Black. "And the Word Became Flesh: Therapeutic Implications for Homiletics in the Later Writings of Ludwig Wittgenstein." Ph.D. diss., Princeton Theological Seminary, 1994.

**424** Johnstone, Araminta Stone. "Theory, Rationality, and Relativism (M. Polanyi, P. Winch, C. Taylor, Wittgenstein and the Azande)." *Tradition and Discovery* 20 (1993): 16-28.

**425** Jones, Joe R. ed. "Colloquy on Kierkegaard, Wittgenstein, and Religious Belief." *Perkins Journal* 24 (1971): 5-38.

**426** Jones, K. "Logic and Science in the *Tractatus.*" *Explorations in Knowledge* 2 (1985): 18-24.

**427** Jones, William Thomas. *A History of Western Philosophy: The Twentieth Century to Wittgenstein and Sartre.* New York: Harcourt Brace Jovanovich, 1975.

**428** Joubert, Jean-Marc. "Ce qu'est un miracle selon L Wittgenstein." *Revue Thomiste* 86 (1986): 115-126.

**429** Junker, Kirk William. "On the Way to Silence from Science (Rhetoric of Science)." Ph.D. diss., University of Pittsburgh, 1996.

**430** Kalansuriya, A. D. P. *A Philosophical Analysis of Buddhist Notions: The Buddha and Wittgenstein.* Delhi: Sri Satguru Publications, 1987.

**431** Kalansuriya, A. D. P. "Wittgenstein's Meaning-Model and Buddhism." *Indian Philosophical Quarterly* 4 (1977): 381-391.

**432** Kalupahana, David. "The Notion of Suffering in Early Buddhism Compared with Some Reflections of Early Wittgenstein." *Philosophy East and West* 27 (1977): 423-431.

**433** Kasachkoff, Tziporah. "Talk About God's Existence." *Philosophical Studies (Ireland)* 19 (1970): 181-192.

**434** Katz, Nathan. "Nagarjuna and Wittgenstein on Error." In *International Seminar on Buddhism's Contribution to World Culture and Civilization*, ed. A. Guruge and D. Ahir, 69-89. New Delhi: Maha Bodhi Society of India, 1977.

435 Kaufman, Gordon D. "Reading Wittgenstein: Notes for Constructive Theologians." *Journal of Religion* 79 (1999): 404-421.

436 Kaufmann, W. *Critique of Religion and Philosophy.* New York: Harper and Row, 1952.

437 Keeling, L. Bryant, and Mario F. Morelli. "Beyond Wittgensteinian Fideism: An Examination of John Hick's Analysis of Religious Faith." *International Journal for Philosophy of Religion* 8 (1977): 250-262.

438 Keightley, Alan. *Into Every Life a Little Zen Must Fall: A Christian Philosopher Looks to Alan Watts and the East.* A Wisdom East-West Book, Grey series. London: Wisdom Publications, 1986.

439 Keightley, Alan. *Wittgenstein, Grammar, and God.* London: Epworth Press, 1976.

440 Kellenberger, James. "Absolute Belief." *Philosophical Investigations* 2 (1979): 1-11.

441 Kellenberger, James. "The Language-Game View of Religion and Religious Certainty." *Canadian Journal of Philosophy* 2 (1972): 255-275.

442 Kellenberger, James. "Wittgenstein and Truth in Incompatible Religious Traditions." *Studies in Religion/Sciences religieuses* 12 (1983): 167-181.

443 Kellenberger, James. "Wittgenstein's Gift to Contemporary Analytic Philosophy of Religion." *International Journal for Philosophy of Religion* 28 (1990): 147-172.

**444** Keller, Joseph. "Ordinary Language Theory and the Return to Metaphysics." *Journal of Religious Studies (Ohio)* 9 (1981): 1-9.

**445** Keller, Joseph. "Theological Linguistics: A Suggestion." *Journal of Religious Studies* 12 (1985): 46-55.

**446** Kelsey, David. *The Uses of Scripture in Recent Theology.* Fortress: Philadelphia, 1975.

**447** Kelsey, David H. "The Bible and Christian Theology." *Journal of the American Academy of Religion* 48 (1980): 385-402.

**448** Kenny, Anthony. "Aquinas and Wittgenstein." *Downside Review* 77 (1959): 217-235.

**449** Kermode, Robert. "Why Scepticism Is Not Reasonable." M.A. thesis, McGill University (Canada), 1990.

**450** Kerr, Fergus. *La teologia dopo Wittgenstein.* Giornale di teologia, 215. Brescia: Queriniana, 1992.

**451** Kerr, Fergus. *La theologie apres Wittgenstein: une introduction a la lecture de Wittgenstein.* Cogitatio Fidei, 162. Paris: Editions Du Cerf, 1991.

**452** Kerr, Fergus. "Metaphysics and Magic: Wittgenstein's Kink." In *Post-Secular Philosophy*, 240-258. London: Routledge, 1998.

**453** Kerr, Fergus. *Theology after Wittgenstein.* 2 ed. London: SPCK, 1997.

454 Kerr, Fergus. "Transubstantiation after Wittgenstein." *Modern Theology* 15 (1999): 115-130.

455 Kerr, Fergus. "What's Wrong with Realism Anyway." In *God and Reality*. London: Mowbray, 1997.

456 Kerr, Fergus. "Wittgenstein and Theological Studies." *New Blackfriars* 63 (1982): 500-508.

457 King-Farlow, John. "Simplicity, Analogy and Plain Religious Lives." *Faith and Philosophy* 1 (1984): 216-229.

458 Kinlaw, C. Jeffery. "De-centering the Autonomous Rational Self: James C. Edwards on the Nonsense of Philosophical Nihilism." *Perspectives in Religious Studies* 18 (1991): 171-180.

459 Kjärgaard, Mogens Stiller. "Metaforen: form og funktion - en formalsemantisk analyse af et principielt fortolkningsproblem." *Dansk Teologisk Tidsskrift* 45 (1982): 225-242.

460 Klinefelter, Donald S. "D. Z. Phillips as Philosopher of Religion." *Journal of the American Academy of Religion* 42 (1974): 307-325.

461 Kowal, Kristopher Hamilton. "The Semantics of Multicultural Discourse: Linguistic Relativity, Contrastive Rhetoric, Intercultural Pragmatics." Ph.D. diss., University of Illinois at Chicago, 1994.

462 Krieg, Gustav A. "Die Rede vom Ende der Rede: Frühe dialektische Theologie und prinzipielle Homiletik." *Zeitschrift für Theologie und Kirche* 94 (1997): 224-252.

463 Kroy, Moshe. "Early Wittgenstein on Death." *Indian Philosophical Quarterley* 9 (1982): 239-244.

464 Kuitert, H. M. "Is Belief a Condition for Understanding?" *Religious Studies* 17 (1981): 233-243.

465 Kurosaki, Hiroshi. *Witogenshutain to Zen.* Tokyo: Tetsugaku Shobo, 1987.

466 Kurten, Tage. *Grunder for en kontextuell teologi: ett wittgensteinskt satt att narma sig teologin i diskussion med Anders Jeffner.* Abo: Abo akademi Distribution, Tidningsbokhandeln (distributor), 1987.

467 Kurtén, Tage. "Glebe-Moller, Wittgenstein og 'Helligånden'." *Dansk Teologisk Tidsskrift* 57 (1994): 116-132.

468 Lachel, Darrel. "Belief from Two Points of View." M.A. thesis, San Diego State University, 1974.

469 Ladrière, Jean. "Athéisme et néopositivisme." In *Des Chretiens interrogent l'athéisme, 2/1: L'Athéisme dans la philosophie contemporaine,* ed. Jean-Prancois Six, 555-621. Paris: Desclée, 1970.

470 Lagache, Agnes. *Wittgenstein: la logique d'un dieu.* Collection Horizon philosophique. Paris: Editions du Cerf, 1975.

471 Langworthy, Robert Stover. "The Certainty of Faith: Wittgenstein's *On Certainty* and Christian Apologetics." Ph.D. diss., Yale University, 1984.

472 Larrimore, Mark. "Honest to God, the Real Wittgenstein: Fergus Kerr's Theology after Wittgenstein." *Koinonia* 3 (1991): 103-130.

**473** Larson, Gerald J. "Prolegomenon to a Theory of Religion." *Journal of the American Academy of Religion* 46 (1978): 443-463.

**474** Lash, Nicholas. *Easter in Ordinary: Relections on Human Experience and the Knowledge of God.* Charlottesville: University Press of Virginia, 1988.

**475** Lash, Nicholas. "How Large is a 'Language Game'?" *Theology* 87 (1984): 19-28.

**476** Laura, Ronald S. "Epistemic Considerations and the Religious Use of Language." *Anglican Theological Review* 52 (1970): 142-150.

**477** Laura, Ronald S. "God, Necessary Exemplification, and the Synthetic/Analytic." *International Journal for Philosophy of Religion* 4 (1973): 119-127.

**478** Laura, Ronald S. "Positivism and Philosophy of Religion." *Sophia* 11 (1972): 13-20.

**479** Laura, Ronald S. "The Positivist Poltergeist and Some Difficulties with Wittgensteinian Liberation." *International Journal for Philosophy of Religion* 2 (1971): 183-190.

**480** Lazerowitz, Morris, and Alice Ambrose. *Philosophical Theories.* The Hague: Mouton, 1976.

**481** Lear, Jonathan. "Moral Objectivity." In *Objectivity and Cultural Divergence*, ed. S. Brown, 135-170. New York: Cambridge University Press, 1984.

**482** Lee-Lampshire, Wendy. "History as Genealogy: Wittgenstein and the Feminist Deconstruction of Objectivity." *Philosophy and Theology* 5 (1991): 313-331.

**483** Leier, Brendan. "Meditations on Wittgenstein's Ethics." M.A. thesis, University Of Alberta, 1994.

**484** Leinfellner, Elisabeth, ed. *Wittgenstein and His Impact on Contemporary Thought: Second International Wittgenstein Symposium, 1977, Kirchberg/Wechsel, Austria.* Vienna: Hölder-Pichler-Tempsky, 1978.

**485** Leinfellner, Werner, and Franz M. Wuketits, eds. *The Tasks of Contemporary Philosophy: Proceedings of the Tenth International Wittgenstein Symposium.* Vienna: Hölder-Pichler-Tempsky, 1986.

**486** Lerner, Berel Dov. "Wittgenstein's Scapegoat." *Philosophical Investigations* 17 (1994): 604-612.

**487** Leuze, Reinhard. "Die Möglichkeiten des Redens von Gott: ein Beitrag zur Lehre von den Eigenschaften Gottes." *Neue Zeitschrift für systematische Theologie und Religionsphilosophie* 26 (1984): 207-217.

**488** Lillegard, Norman. "Understanding and Believing." Ph.D. diss., The University of Nebraska - Lincoln, 1981.

**489** Lillegard, Norman. "Wittgenstein on Primitive Religion." In *Philosophy of Religion,* ed. W. Gombocz, 170-172. Vienna: Hölder-Pichler-Tempsky, 1984.

**490** Lindbeck, George. *The Nature of Doctrine: Religion and Theology in a Postliberal Age.* Philadelphia: Westminster, 1984.

**491** Lippitt, John, and Daniel D. Hutto. "Making Sense of Nonsense: Kierkegaard and Wittgenstein." *Proceedings of the Aristotelian Society* 98 (1998): 263-286.

**492**  Liverziani, F. "L'Esperienza metafisico-religiosa de fronte al neopositivismo." *Aquinas: Rivista Internazionale di Filosofia* 14 (1971): 369-380.

**493**  Loades, Ann. "Moral Sentiment and Belief in God (in the work of Kant)." *Studia Theologica* 35 (1981): 72-83.

**494**  Loehr, Davidson. "The Legitimate Heir to Theology: A Study of Ludwig Wittgenstein." Ph.D. diss., University of Chicago, Divinity School, 1988.

**495**  Long, Charles H. "Silence and Signification: A Note on Religion and Modernity." In *Myths and Symbols: Studies in Honor of Mircea Eliade*, ed. J. M. Kitagawa, 141-150. Chicago: University of Chicago Press, 1969.

**496**  Lucier, Pierre. "Le statut du language religieux dans la philosophie de Ludwig Wittgenstein." *Studies in Religion/ Sciences religieuses* 3 (1973): 14-28.

**497**  Luijpen, Wilhelmus Antonius. *Theology as Anthropology: Philosophical Reflections on Religion.* New York: Humanities Press, 1973.

**498**  Lujan-Martinez, Horacio. "William James and His Influence on the Wittgenstenian Mysticism [in Spanish]." *Revista de Filosofia Venezuela* 30 (1998): 87-105.

**499**  MacIntyre, Alasdair, ed. *Metaphysical Beliefs: Three Essays.* London: SCM Press, 1970.

**500**  Macquarrie, John. *God-Talk: An Examination of the Language and Logic of Theology.* London: SCM Press, 1967.

**501**  Madden, E. H., and P. H. Hare. "On the Difficulty of Evading the Problem of Evil." *Philosophy and Phenomenolical Research* 28 (1967): 58-69.

**502**  Maesschalck, Marc. "Le problème du discours éthique, de Lévy-Bruhl à Wittgenstein." *Science et Esprit* 43 (1991): 187-204.

**503**  Maesschalck, Marc. "Métaphysique et éthique chez Wittgenstein: à propos d'un ouvrage récent." *Science et Esprit* 42 (1990): 103-109.

**504**  Magee, Bryan, ed. *Modern British Philosophy.* London: Secker and Warburg, 1971.

**505**  Magnanini, Dina. *Il pensiero religioso di Ludwig Wittgenstein.* Rome: La Goliardica, 1981.

**506**  Magnanini, Dina. "Tolstoj E. Wittgenstein come 'Imitatori di Cristo'." *Sapienza* 32 (1979): 89-100.

**507**  Magnus, Bernd. "Postmodern Pragmatism: Nietzsche, Heidegger, Derrida, and Rorty." In *Pragmatism: From Progressivism to Postmodernism*, ed. Robert Hollinger. Westport: Praeger, 1995.

**508**  Malcolm, Norman. *Wittgenstein: A Religious Point of View? (Edited and with a Response by Peter Winch).* Ithaca: Cornell University Press, 1994.

**509**  Marini, Sergio. *Etica e religione nel 'primo Wittgenstein'.* Scienze filosofiche, 42. Milano: Vita e pensiero, 1989.

**510**  Marini, Sergio. "La presenza di Kierkegaard nel pensiero di Wittgenstein." *Revista di Filosofia Neo-Scolastica* 78 (1986): 211-226.

**511** Mark, James. "Wittgenstein and Theology." *Theology* 85 (1982): 321-324.

**512** Martin, Dean. "Christian Consciousness: Its Emergence with the Mastery of Concepts within the Christian Community— With Special Reference to Ludwig Wittgenstein." Ph.D. diss., Baylor University, 1972.

**513** Martin, Dean. "God and Objects: Beginning with Existence." *International Journal for Philosophy of Religion* 41 (1997): 1-11.

**514** Martin, Dean. "Language, Theology and the Subject Life." *Perspectives in Religious Studies* 5 (1978): 184-194.

**515** Martin, Dean. "Language, Thinking and Religious Conscious-ness." *International Journal for Philosophy of Religion* 10 (1979): 163-176.

**516** Martin, Dean. "Learning to Become a Christian." *Religious Education* 82 (1987): 94-114.

**517** Martin, Dean. "*On Certainty* and Religious Belief." *Religious Studies* 20 (1984): 593-614.

**518** Martin, Glen T. "The Religious Nature of Wittgenstein's Later Philosophy." *Philosophy Today* 32 (1988): 207-220.

**519** Martin, James Alfred. "Collingwood and Wittgenstein on the Task of Philosophy." *Philosophy Today* 25 (1981): 12-23.

**520** Martin, James Alfred. *The New Dialogue between Philosophy and Theology.* New York: Seabury Press, 1966.

**521** Martin, Michael. "Wittgenstein's Lectures on Religious Be-lief." *Heythrop Journal* 32 (1991): 369-382.

**522** Martinich, A. P. "Unspeakable Acts: A Reply to Brinkman." *Heythrop Journal* 17 (1976): 188-189.

**523** Mattingly, Byron Mark. "Measure and Skepticism in Wittgenstein's Philosophy of Language." Ph.D. diss., State University of New York At Stony Brook, 1995.

**524** Maurer, Ernstpeter. "Biblisches Reden von Gott: ein Sprachspiel? Anmerkungen zu einem Vergleich von Karl Barth und Ludwig Wittgenstein." *Evangelische Theologie* 50 (1990): 71-82.

**525** McCabe, Herbert. "The Logic of Mysticism." *Philosophy* 31 (1992): 45-59.

**526** McCarthy, G. "Newman and Wittgenstein: The Problem of Certainty." *Irish Theological Quarterly* 49 (1982): 98-120.

**527** McClendon, James, and Brad J. Kallenberg. "Ludwig Wittgenstein: A Christian in Philosophy." *Scottish Journal of Theology* 51 (1998): 131-161.

**528** McDermott, Robert A. "Religion Game: Some Family Resemblances." *Journal of the American Academy of Religion* 38 (1970): 390-400.

**529** McDonald, Henry. *The Normative Basis of Culture: A Philosophical Inquiry.* Baton Rouge: Louisiana University Press, 1986.

**530** McFarlane, Adrian Anthony. *A Grammar of Fear and Evil: A Husserlian-Wittgensteinian Hermeneutic.* New York: Lang, 1996.

**531** McGhee, Michael. "The Locations of the Soul." *Religious Studies* 32 (1996): 205-221.

**532** McGuinness, Brian. "Freud and Wittgenstein." In *Wittgenstein and His Times*, ed. B. McGuinness, 27-43. Chicago: University of Chicago Press, 1982.

**533** McGuinness, Brian. "The Mysticism of the *Tractatus.*" *The Philosophical Review* 75 (1966): 305-328.

**534** McHale, Mary Elwyn. "The Notion of the Mystical in Wittgenstein's *Tractatus.*" Ph.D. diss., Catholic University of America, 1979.

**535** McKnight, Terence J. "Wittgenstein and the Miraculous." In *Philosophy of Religion*, ed. W. Gombocz, 161-163. Vienna: Hölder-Pichler-Tempsky, 1984.

**536** McLaughlin, Paul. "Wittgenstein and Moral Knowledge." *Downside Review* 105 (1987): 12-22.

**537** McLaughlin, Terence H. "Wittgenstein, Education, and Religion." *Studies in Philosophy of Religion* 14 (1995): 295-311.

**538** McLean, Malcolm D. "The Meaning of Sunya in the Teaching of Nagarjuna (Four Views)." *Scottish Journal of Religious Studies* 7 (1986): 29-50.

**539** McNulty, T. Michael. "Reflections on Religious Language." *The New Scholasticism* 49 (1975): 127-139.

**540** McPherson, Thomas. "Positivism and Religion." *Philosophy and Phenomenological Research* 14 (1954): 319-331.

**541** Meynell, Hugo A. "Lonergan, Wittgenstein, and Where Language Hooks onto the World." In *Creativity and Method: Essays in Honor of Bernard Lonergan*, ed. M. Lamb, 369-381. Milwaukee: Marquette University Press, 1981.

**542** Midgley, Mary. "The Game Game." *Philosophy* 49 (1974): 231-253.

**543** Miller, Alexander. "Sublimination, Realism, and Rule-Following: An Outline of a Humanized Platonism: Ludwig Wittgenstein, Crispin Wright, John McDowell." Ph.D. diss., The University of Michigan, 1995.

**544** Miller, Caleb. "The Later Wittgenstein and Religious Belief." Thesis (M.A.T.S.), Gordon-Conwell Theological Seminary, 1983.

**545** Miller, James Bradley. "Beyond Dualism: Cosmological Issues for Christian Theology in a Post-Modern, Post-Critical Cultural Context." Ph.D. diss., Marquette University, 1986.

**546** Miller, Libuse Lukas. *Knowing, Doing, and Surviving: Cognition in Evolution.* Chichester: Wiley-Interscience, 1973.

**547** Moen, Arthur J. "Paradigms, Language Games, and Religious Belief." *Christian Scholar's Review* 9 (1979): 17-29.

**548** Mojtabai, A. G. "Linguistic Analysis and Religious Language." *Philosophy Today* 2 (1967): 60-71.

**549** Møller, Jens Glebe. "Om bestemmelsen af etiske saetninger ifølge Wittgensteins *Tractatus.*" *Svensk Teologisk Kvartalskrift* 44 (1968): 96-104.

550 Mondin, Battista. "Il linguaggio teologico espressione del misterio rivelato nel linguaggio umano." *Sapienza* 46 (1993): 241-262.

551 Mood, John J. "Poetic Languaging and Primal Thinking: A Study of Barfield, Wittgenstein, and Heidegger." *Encounter* 26 (1965): 417-433.

552 Moore, Gareth. *Believing in God: A Philosophical Essay.* Edinburgh: Clark, 1988.

553 Moore, Gareth, and Brian Davies. "Philosophy and Religion: Wittgenstein and the Philosophy of Religion." In *Philosophy of Religion*, ed. Brian Davies. Washington: Georgetown University Press, 1998.

554 Moore, J.M. "Analytical Philosophy and Its Bearing upon Theology." *Journal of Religious Thought* 17 (1960): 87-100.

555 Moore, Robert W. "The Concept of Religion." In *Church Divinity: National Student Essay Competition in Divinity, 1981*, ed. J. Morgan, 81-88. Notre Dame, IN: Parish Church Library, 1981.

556 Moran, Patrick. "Pascal and Wittgenstein: Common Epistemological Elements in the *Pensées* and *On Certainty* (Ludwig Wittgenstein, Blaise Pascal, G. E. Moore, René Descartes)." M.A. thesis, University of Ottawa, 1997.

557 Morot-Sir, Edouard. *Pascal Versus Wittgenstein, with Samuel Beckett as the Anti-Witness.* Chapel Hill, N.C.: University of North Carolina, 1974.

558 Morse, Christopher L. "Raising God's Eyebrows: Some Further Thoughts on the Concept of the analogia fidei." *Union Seminary Quarterly Review* 37 (1982): 39-49.

559 Mullin, Albert Alkins. *Philosophical Comments on the Philosophies of Charles Sanders Peirce and Ludwig Wittgenstein.* Urbana: University of Illinois, 1961.

560 Munz, Regine. *Religion als Beispiel: Sprache und Methode bei Ludwig Wittgenstein in theologischer Perspektive.* Dusseldorf: Parerga Verlag, 1997.

561 Murphy, Francesca. "Fergus Kerr's Wittgensteinian 'Philosophy of Theology': An Appreciation and a Critique." *Scottish Journal of Theology* 45 (1992): 449-463.

562 Murphy, John James. "Mysticism and Epistemology: A Study and Comparison of Modern Philosophical Analyses of Mysticism and the Thought of Ludwig Wittgenstein." Ph.D. diss., The Claremont Graduate University, 1995.

563 Muyskens, James L. "Religious-Belief as Hope." *International Journal for Philosophy of Religion* 5 (1974): 246-253.

564 Nebreda, J. J. "Para una historia de las 'muertes de Dios': De Newton a Wittgenstein." *Pensamiento* 198 (1994): 471-488.

565 Needham, Rodney. *Belief, Language, and Experience.* Oxford: Blackwell, 1972.

566 Nepomechie, Esther Adouth. "Skepticism: An Overview (Epistemology, Naturalism)." Ph.D. diss., University of Miami, 1993.

567 Nevo, Isaac. "Religious Belief and Jewish Identity in Wittgenstein's Philosophy." *Philosophy Research Archives* 13 (1987): 225-243.

**568** Newman, Elizabeth. "Alexander Schmemann and Orthodox Theology: The Liturgy as Sacred Sprachspiel." Ph.D. diss., Duke University, 1990.

**569** Newport, John P. "Representative Contemporary Approaches to the Use of Philosophy in Christian Thought." *Review and Expositor* 82 (1985): 507-519.

**570** Nicholson, Michael W. "Abusing Wittgenstein: The Misuse of the Concept of Language Games in Contemporary Theology: Critique of Lindbeck, Thiselton, Wright." *Journal of the Evangelical Theological Society* 39 (1996): 617-629.

**571** Nicolet, Daniel. "Langage et raison: philosophie, linguistique et ce qui leur ressemble." *Revue de Théologie et de Philosophie* 121 (1989): 353-375.

**572** Niedballa, Thomas. *Christliches Sprachspiel und religiose Erfahrung: Wittgenstein und die Theologie. Studien zur systematischen Theologie und Ethik*, Bd. 3. Munster: Lit, 1993.

**573** Nieli, Russell. *Wittgenstein: From Mysticism to Ordinary Language: A Study of Viennese Positivism and the Thought of Ludwig Wittgenstein.* Albany: State University of New York Press, 1987.

**574** Nielsen, Harry. "Kierkegaard's Metaphysical Crotchet." *Proceedings of the American Catholic Philosophical Association* 46 (1972): 123-130.

**575** Nielsen, Harry. "A Meeting of Minds on Water." In *The Grammar of the Heart: New Essays in Moral Philosophy and Theology*, ed. R. Bell, 75-82. San Francisco: Harper and Row, 1988.

**576** Nielsen, Harry. "Some Wrinkles in the Religious Uses of 'to Believe'." *Philosophy Research Archives* 2 (1976).

**577** Nielsen, Kai. "The Challenge of Wittgenstein: An Examination of His Picture of Religious Belief." *Studies in Religion/Sciences religieuses* 3 (1973): 29-46.

**578** Nielsen, Kai. "The Coherence of Wittgensteinian Fideism." *Sophia* 11 (1972): 4-12.

**579** Nielsen, Kai. "God, Disembodied Existence and Incoherence." *Sophia (Australia)* 26 (1987): 27-52.

**580** Nielsen, Kai. *God, Scepticism and Modernity.* Ottawa: University of Ottawa Press, 1989.

**581** Nielsen, Kai. *An Introduction to the Philosophy of Religion.* New York: St. Martin's Press, 1982.

**582** Nielsen, Kai. "On Mucking Around About God: Some Methodological Animadversions." *International Journal for Philosophy of Religion* 16 (1984): 111-122.

**583** Nielsen, Kai. "Religion and Groundless Believing." In *Religious Experience and Religious Belief,* ed. Joseph Runzo. Lanham, MD: University Press of America, 1986.

**584** Nielsen, Kai. "Religion and Groundless Believing." In *The Autonomy of Religious Belief,* ed. F. Crosson, 93-107. Notre Dame: University of Notre Dame Press, 1981.

**585** Nielsen, Kai. "Religion and the Appeal to Forms of Life." *Agora* 3 (1975-1976): 67-71.

**586** Nielsen, Kai. *Scepticism.* London: Macmillan, 1973.

**587** Nielsen, Kai. "Wisdom and Dilman and the Reality of God." *Religious Studies* 16 (1980): 49-60.

**588** Nielsen, Kai. "Wittgensteinian Fideism." *Philosophy* 42 (1967): 191-209.

**589** Nielsen, Kai. "Wittgensteinian Fideism." In *Contemporary Philosophy of Religion*, ed. S. Cahn, 237-254. New York: Oxford University Press, 1982.

**590** Nielsen, Kai. "Wittgensteinian Fideism Again, a Reply to Hudson." *Philosophy* 44 (1969): 63-65.

**591** Nielson, Kai. *Contemporary Critique of Religion*. London: Macmillan, 1972.

**592** Nielson, Kai. "On the Rationality of Groundless Believing." *Idealistic Studies* 11 (1981): 215-229.

**593** Norris, Frederick W. "Theology as Grammar: Nazianzen and Wittgenstein." In *Arianism after Arius*, ed. Michel Barnes and Daniel Williams, 237-249. Edinburgh: T & T Clark, 1993.

**594** Northrop, F. S. C. "Language, Mysticism and God." In *Man, Nature and God*, ed. F. S. C. Northrop, 238-245. New York: Simon and Schuster, 1962.

**595** Nuechterlien, John David. "The Conceptual Theory of Meaning: God, the World, and Everything (Ludwig Wittgenstein, Martin Heidegger)." Ph.D. diss., University of Miami, 1995.

**596** Nystrand, Stig. "When God Was Absent." In *The Tasks of Contemporary Philosophy*, ed. Werner Leinfellner. Vienna: Hölder-Pichler-Tempsky, 1986.

**597** Nystrand, Stig. "Wittgenstein and Jaspers: How to Live in Borderlands." In *Philosophy of Religion*, ed. W. Gombocz, 190-195. Vienna: Hölder-Pichler-Tempsky, 1984.

**598** Oakes, Edward T. "Ludwig Wittgenstein Confesses." *First Things* (1992): 37-41.

**599** O'Callaghan, John Patrick Thomas. "Mental Representation: St. Thomas and the 'De Interpretatione'." Ph.D. diss., University of Notre Dame, 1996.

**600** O'Connor, Margaret Rose. "Back to the Rough Ground: Wittgensteinian Moral Realism (Ludwig Josef Johan Wittgenstein)." Ph.D. diss., University Of Minnesota, 1996.

**601** O'Hear, Anthony. "Statements of Religious Belief." *Religious Studies* 14 (1978): 361-372.

**602** O'Hear, Anthony. "Wittgenstein's Method of Perspicuous Representation and the Study of Religion." In *Wittgenstein and His Impact*, ed. E. Leinfellner, 521-524. Vienna: Hölder-Pichler-Tempsky, 1978.

**603** O'Keeffe, Terence M. "Comprendre la religion: remarques sur la philosophie anglophone contemporaine de la religion." *Revue des sciences philosophiques et théologiques* 64 (1980): 531-546.

**604** Olmsted, Richard. "Wittgenstein and Christian Truth Claims." *Scottish Journal of Theology* 33 (1980): 121-132.

**605** Ommen, Thomas B. "Wittgensteinian Fideism and Theology." *Horizons* 7 (1980): 183-204.

**606** Ott, Heinrich. "Philosophical Theology as Confrontation." In *The Future of Philosophical Theology*, ed. R. Evans, 144-168. Philadelphia: Westminster Press, 1971.

**607** Otubanjo, Femi. "Wittgensteinianism and Magico-Religious Beliefs." *Theoria to Theory* 13 (1979): 149-162.

**608** Palma, A. "Religious Icons, Prayers and Practices." *Sophia (Australia)* 27 (1988): 26-39.

**609** Palmer, Anthony. "Violations of Nature and Conditions of Sense." In *Philosophy and the Grammar of Religious Belief*, ed. T. Tessin, 186-199. New York: St. Martin's Press, 1995.

**610** Paltrinieri, Gian Luigi. "Kant, Wittgenstein e l'argomento ontologico." *Teoria* 11 (1991): 105-130.

**611** Parret, Herman. "Introduction: Beliefs and Believing: the Web and the Spinning." In *On Believing*, ed. H. Parret, 1-15. Berlin: W. de Gruyter, 1983.

**612** Parret, Herman. "Wittgenstein Ii Bis." *Tijdsch Filosof* 45 (1983): 261-290.

**613** Paterno, Joseph William. "The Argument from Contingency: The Metaphysical Approaches of Bradley and Royce in Comparison with the Analytic Approach (F. H. Bradley, Josiah Royce)." M.A. thesis, The American University, 1995.

**614** Patterson, Sue. "Gratuitous Truth: Metaphor and Revelation." *Colloquium* 24 (1992): 29-43.

**615** Patterson, Sue. "Word, Words and World." *Colloquium* 23 (1991): 71-84.

**616** Patt-Shamir, Galia. "The Riddle of Confucianism: The Case of Tongshu (Zhou Dunyi, Eleventh Century)." Ph.D. diss., Harvard University, 1997.

**617** Pellecchia, Pasquale. "L'esilio ou-topico dell'etica: L Wittgenstein." *Aquinas* 37 (1994): 523-545.

**618** Pence, Terry. "Ludwig Wittgenstein: The Bearing of his Thought upon the Issues of Religious Language and Belief." M.A. thesis, Trinity Evangelical Divinity School, 1974.

**619** Penco, Carlo. "Gottlob Frege, lettere a Wittgenstein." *Epistemologia* (1989): 331-351.

**620** Penelhum, Terence. "Sceptics, Believers, and Historical Mistakes." *Synthese* 67 (1986): 131-146.

**621** Peregrin, Jaroslav. "Language and the World (in Czechoslovakian)." *Filozoficky Casopis* 41 (1993): 737-760.

**622** Perrett, Roy W. "Solipsism and Religious Belief." *Sophia* 20 (1981): 17-26.

**623** Petersen, Michael. "Theology and Linguistic Analysis in the 20th Century." *Wesleyan Theological Journal* 15 (1980): 19-33.

**624** Peterson, Thomas D. *Wittgenstein for Preaching: A Model for Communication.* Lanham, MD: University Press of America, 1980.

**625** Petri, Jean Bernhard. "Ludwig Wittgenstein und der mathematische Grundlagenstreit." *Zeitschrift für Katholische Theologie* 106 (1984): 503-504.

**626** Phillips, D. Z. *Belief, Change and Forms of Life.* Atlantic Highlands: Humanities Press, 1986.

**627** Phillips, D. Z. "Belief, Change, and Forms of Life: The Confusions of Externalism and Internalism." In *The Autonomy of Religious Belief,* ed. F. Crosson, 60-92. Notre Dame: University of Notre Dame Press, 1981.

**628** Phillips, D. Z. *The Concept of Prayer.* London: Routledge & Kegan Paul, 1965.

**629** Phillips, D. Z. *Death and Immortality.* London: Macmillan, 1970.

**630** Phillips, D. Z. "Dislocating the Soul: Reply by John Hyman." In *Can Religion Be Explained Away?,* ed. D. Z. Phillips, 233-251. New York: St. Martin's Press, 1996.

**631** Phillips, D. Z. *Faith after Foundationalism.* London: Routledge, 1988.

**632** Phillips, D. Z. *Faith and Philosophical Enquiry.* London: Routledge and Kegan Paul, 1970.

**633** Phillips, D. Z. "On Giving Practice Its Due: A Reply." *Religious Studies* 31 (1995): 121-127.

**634** Phillips, D.Z. "On Wanting to Compare Wittgenstein and Zen." *Philosophy* 52 (1977): 338-343.

**635** Phillips, D. Z. "Primitive Reactions and the Reactions of Primitives: The 1983 Marett Lecture." *Religious Studies* 22 (1986): 165-180.

**636** Phillips, D. Z. "Religion in Wittgenstein's Mirror." In *Wittgenstein Centenary Essays*, ed. A Phillips Griffiths. New York: Cambridge University Press, 1991.

**637** Phillips, D. Z. *Religion Without Explanation*. Oxford: Basil Blackwell, 1976.

**638** Phillips, D. Z. "Religion, Philosophy, and the Academy." *International Journal for Philosophy of Religion* 44 (1998): 129-144.

**639** Phillips, D. Z. "Religious Beliefs and Language Games." *Ratio* 12 (1970): 26-46.

**640** Phillips, D. Z. "Searle on Language Games and Religion." *Tijdschrift voor Filosofie* 51 (1989): 245-255.

**641** Phillips, D. Z. "Voices in Discussion." In *Philosophy and the Grammar of Religious Belief*, ed. T. Tessin, 367-393. New York: St. Martin's Press, 1995.

**642** Phillips, D. Z. *Wittgenstein and Religion*. New York: St. Martin's Press, 1993.

**643** Phillips, D. Z. "Wittgenstein's Full Stop." In *Perspectives on the Philosophy of Wittgenstein*, ed. I Block, 179-200. Oxford: Blackwell, 1981.

**644** Phillips, D. Z., and J. R. Jones. "Belief and Loss of Belief: A Discussion." *Sophia* 9 (1970): 1-7.

**645** Phillips, D. Z., and Peter Winch, eds. *Wittgenstein: Attention to Particulars: Essays in Honour of Rush Rhees*. London: Macmillan, 1989.

646  Pierre, Jacques. "L'impasse de la définition de la religion: analyse et dépassement." *Religiologiques* (1994): 15-29.

647  Pititto, Rocco. *La fede come passione: Ludwig Wittgenstein e la religione.* Universo filosofia, Saggi, 23. Cinisello Balsamo (Milano): San Paolo, 1997.

648  Placher, William C. *Unapologetic Theology: A Christian Voice in a Pluralistic Conversation.* Louisville: Westminster, 1989.

649  Poling, John David. "Subjective Thinking in Kierkegaard's Thought (Ludwig Wittgenstein, Ethics)." Ph.D. diss., Vanderbilt University, 1996.

650  Polish, David. "Towards a Progressive Theology of Zionism." *Judaism* 26 (1977): 489-498.

651  Popov, Stefan Georgiev. "Wittgenstein's Analytic of the Mystical (Ethics, Aesthetics)." Ph.D. diss., New School for Social Research, 1997.

652  Porter, Stanley E. "Wittgenstein's Classes of Utterances and Pauline Ethical Texts." *Journal of the Evangelical Theological Society* 32 (1989): 85-97.

653  Portmann, Franz. "Glaubenslose Religion und Glaubensreligion." *Conceptus* 20 (1986): 69-78.

654  Portmann, Franz. "Religion und Vernunft: Eine Rekonstruktion von Wittgensteins Religionphilosophie." *Studia Philosophica (Switzerland)* 45 (1986): 127-151.

655  Pouivet, Roger. *Apres Wittgenstein, Saint Thomas.* Philosophies, 93. Paris: Presses Universitaires de France, 1997.

**656** Poulain, Jacques. "Le mysticisme du Tractatus Logico-Philosophicus et la situation paradoxale des propositions religieuses." In *La recherche en philosophie*, ed. D. Dubarle, 75-155. Paris: Editions du Cerf, 1970.

**657** Poulain, Jacques. *Logique et religion. L'atomisme logique de L. Wittgenstein et la possibilite des propositions religieuses. Suivi de Logic and religion. A shortened and adapted version.* Religion and reason, 7. La Haye, Paris: Mouton, 1973.

**658** Poupore, Delilah A. "Appling Wittgenstein to the Question of Multiculturalism in the University: Rotating the Axis of Reference about the Fixed Point of Our Real Need." Thesis (M. Ed.), University of Vermont, 1993.

**659** Power, William L. "Analysis and Theology." *Sophia* 17 (1978): 16-26.

**660** Power, William L. "Musings on the Mystery of God." *International Journal for Philosophy of Religion* 7 (1976): 300-310.

**661** Pradhan, R. C. "Life, Will and the World: Some Reflections on the Notebooks 1914-1916." *Journal of Indian Council of Philosophical Research* 10 (1993): 31-47.

**662** Prado, Jose Hernandez. "Max Weber y la racionalizacion, desmagificacion y remagificacion del mundo." *Topicos* 4 (1994): 7-17.

**663** Priestley, Jack. "Teaching Transcendence." In *Religious Education and the Imagination*, ed. M. Tickner and D. Webster, 5-21. Hull: University of Hull, Institute of Education, 1982.

**664** Priestley, Jack Greaves. "Moral Education and Religious Story: An Essay in Support of Whitehead's Contention that the Essence of Education Is that It Be Religious." Ph.D. diss., University of Exeter (United Kingdom), 1988.

**665** Proudfoot, Wayne L. "Religious Experience, Emotion, and Belief." *American Academy of Religion Philosophy of Religion and Theology* (1976).

**666** Puelles, Andoni Alonso. "Tolstoi y Wittgenstein: Una Nueva Encrucijada Religiosa." *Euridice* (1993): 9-51.

**667** Punzo, Vincent C. "Wittgenstein and Philosophy of Religion." In *History of Philosophy in the Making: A Symposium of Essays to Honor Professor James D. Collins on His 65th Birthday*, ed. Linus J. Thro. Washington, D.C.: University Press of America, 1982.

**668** Purtill, Richard L. "Intelligibility of Disembodied Survival." *Christian Scholar's Review* 5 (1975): 3-22.

**669** Putnam, Hilary. "Wittgenstein on Religious Belief." In *On Community*, ed. L. Rouner, 56-75. Notre Dame: University of Notre Dame Press, 1991.

**670** Putti, Joseph. "Grammar of Dogma: An Enquiry into the Nature and Function of Dogma in the Light of Ludwig Wittgenstein's Linguistic Analysis with Special Reference to the Dogma of Chalcedon." Thesis (S.T.L.), Pontifical University, St. Patrick's College, Maynooth, 1982.

**671** Quinn, Wylie Savanas, III. "Kierkegaard and Wittgenstein: The 'Religious' as a 'Form of Life.'." Ph.D. diss., Duke University, 1976.

**672**  Radford, Colin. "Religious Belief and Contradiction." *Philosophy* 50 (1975): 437-444.

**673**  Ralls, Mark. "Wittgenstein's Ancient City: Intersubjective Meaning and the Question of Fideism." *Koinonia* 8 (1996): 32-56.

**674**  Raschke, Carl. "Meaning and Saying in Religion: Beyond Language Games." *Harvard Theological Review* 67 (1974): 79-116.

**675**  Raschke, Carl A. "Paul Ricoeur and Religious Language: From Lebensform to Work of Discourse." *Iliff Review* 35 (1978): 59-64.

**676**  Raschke, Carl A. "Revelation and Conversion: A Semantic Appraisal." *Anglican Theological Review* 60 (1978): 420-436.

**677**  Ray, Rickey Joe. "Crossed Fingers and Praying Hands: Remarks on Religious Belief and Superstition." *Religious Studies* (1990): 471-482.

**678**  Ray, Rickey Joe. "Forms of Life and Religious Belief in the Thought of Wittgenstein and His Interpreters: Alternative Visions of Religion in Society." Ph.D. diss., The Southern Baptist Theological Seminary, 1988.

**679**  Ray, Rickie Joe. "Rendering Judgment on Wittgenstein's 'Last Judgment'." *Encounter* 51 (1990): 209-225.

**680**  Reese, William L. "Religious 'Seeing-as'." *Religious Studies* 14 (1978): 73-87.

**681**  Reiser, Oliver L. "The Role of Symbols in Human Existence." *Main Currents* 25 (1969): 134-142.

**682**  Rhees, Rush. *Without Answers.* London: Routledge & K Paul, 1969.

**683**  Rhees, Rush. "Wittgenstein on Language and Ritual: Discussion of Beltane Fire-Festival of 18th Century Scotland." In *Wittgenstein and His Times,* ed. B. McGuinness, 69-107. Chicago: University of Chicago Press, 1982.

**684**  Richards, Glynn. "Conceptions of the Self in Wittgenstein, Hume, and Buddhism: An Analysis and Comparison." *Monist* 61 (1978): 42-55.

**685**  Richards, Glyn. "Wittgensteinian Approach to the Philosophy of Religion: A Critical Evaluation of D. Z. Phillips." *Journal of Religion* 58 (1978): 288-302.

**686**  Richmond, James. *Theology and Metaphysics.* London: SCM Press, 1970.

**687**  Roberts, H. R. T. "The Concept of 'Seeing-As' In Wittgenstein's Philosophy of Religion." *Indian Philosophical Quarterly* 7 (1979): 71-82.

**688**  Roberts, Robert. *Faith, Reason, and History: Rethinking Kierkegaard's Philosophical Fragments.* Macon: Mercer University Press, 1986.

**689**  Roberts, Robert. "Feeling of Absolute Dependence." *Journal of Religion* 57 (1977): 252-266.

**690**  Robinson, Norman H. G. "After Wittgenstein." *Religious Studies* 12 (1976): 493-507.

**691**  Rollefson, Richard Griffith. "Thinking With Kierkegaard and Wittgenstein: The Philosophical Theology of Paul L. Holmer." Ph.D. diss., Graduate Theological Union, 1994.

**692** Romerales, Enrique, ed. *Creenciay racionalidad: lecturas de filosofía de la religión.* Barcelona: Anthropos, 1992.

**693** Rorty, Richard. "Wittgenstein, Heidegger, and the Reification of Language." In *The Cambridge Companion to Heidegger*, ed. C. Guignon, 337-357. Cambridge: Cambridge University Press, 1993.

**694** Rotella, Oscar. "Santo Tomás y Wittgenstein." *Revista de Filosofía (Mexico)* 8 (1975): 301-317.

**695** Rowe, William L., and William J. Wainwright. *Philosophy of Religion: Selected Readings.* San Diego: Harcourt Brace Jov, 1989.

**696** Rudebush, Thomas, and William M. Berg. "On Wittgenstein and Ethics: Reply to Levi." *Telos* (1979): 150-159.

**697** Rudy, Mary Kathy. "Mapping the Moralities of Abortion (Religious Ethics, Feminism)." Ph.D. diss., Duke University, 1993.

**698** Ruf, Henry. "The Origin of the Debate over Ontotheology and Deconstruction in the Texts of Wittgenstein and Derrida." In *Religion, Ontotheology and Deconstruction*, ed. H. Ruf, 3-42. New York: Paragon House, 1989.

**699** Ryan, John Kenneth, ed. *Twentieth Century Thinkers: Studies in the Work of Seventeen Modern Philosophers.* Staten Island, NY: Alba House, 1965.

**700** Ryder, John Joseph. "Ordinality, Language-Games and Sunyata: Their Implications for Religion." Ph.D. diss., State University of New York at Stony Brook, 1982.

**701** Sachs, David. "On Wittgenstein's *Remarks On Frazer's Golden Bough*." *Philosophical Investigations* 11 (1988): 47-150.

**702** Saliers, Don. *The Soul in Paraphrase: Prayer and the Religious Affections.* New York: Seabury, 1980.

**703** Sarot, Marcel. "Meaning and Life (in Dutch)." *Bijdragen* 54 (1993): 162-176.

**704** Satris, Stephen A. "Wittgenstein and the Philosophy of Religion." In *Wittgenstein and His Impact on Contemporary Thought*, ed. E. Leinfellner, 507-509. Vienna: Hölder-Pichler-Tempsky, 1978.

**705** Saunders, Lloyd W. "Theological Consequences of Philosophy as Immediacy." *American Academy of Religion, Philosophy of Religion Proceedings* (1976): 255-264.

**706** Savigny, Eike von, and Oliver R. Scholz, eds. *Wittgenstein über die Seele*, Suhrkamp-Taschenbuch Wissenschaft, 1173. Frankfurt am Main: Suhrkamp, 1995.

**707** Sayre, Kenneth. "A Perceptual Model of Belief in God." In *The Autonomy of Religious Belief*, ed. Frederick Crosson. Notre Dame: University of Notre Dame Press, 1981.

**708** Sbisà, Marina. "Some Remarks on Belief, Confidence, and Cooperation." In *On Believing: Epistemological and Semiotic Approaches*, ed. H. Parret, 302-315. Berlin: W. de Gruyter, 1983.

**709** Scharfstein, Ben-Ami. "Salvation by Paradox: On Zen and Zen-Like Thought." *Journal of Chinese Philosophy* 3 (1976): 209-234.

710 Schedler, Norbert O. "Talk About God-Talk: A Historical Introduction." In *Philosophy of Religion*, ed. Norbert O. Schedler, 221-250. New York: Macmillan, 1974.

711 Scheier, Claus A. "Wittgenstein und das Schweigen im intentionalen Denken." In *Probleme philosophischer Mystik: Festschrift für Karl Albert zum siebzigsten Geburtstag*, ed. E. Jain R Margreiter, 159-171. Sankt Augustin: Academia Verlag, 1991.

712 Schmidt, Claudia Maria. "Tillich, Gadamer and Wittgenstein on the Idea of Understanding." M.A. thesis, University of California, Santa Barbara, 1985.

713 Schner, George Peter. "The Language of Transcendence." Ph.D. diss., Yale University, 1980.

714 Schroeder, John William. "Nagarjuna's Unsurpassed Medicine: Emptiness and the Doctrine of Upaya (Buddhism)." Ph.D. diss., University of Oregon, 1996.

715 Schweidler, Walter. "Die Ethik des Augenblicks: Jaspers, Kierkegaard, Wittgenstein." In *Karl Jaspers*, ed. R. Wisser, 202-214. Wurzburg: Konigshausen and Neumann, 1993.

716 Schweizer-Bjelic, Shelley, and Dusan I. Bjelic. "God-Talk as 'Tacit' Theo-Logic: Expletive Use of God as Tacit Theology, Wittgensteinian Analysis." *Modern Theology* 6 (1990): 341-366.

717 Scobel, Gert F. "Ludwig Wittgenstein and the Interpretation of New Testament Parables." M.A. Thesis, Jesuit School of Theology at Berkeley/Graduate Theological Union, 1981.

**718** Scott, Jamie S., and Paul Simpson-Housley. "Afterword: The Geographics of Religion in a Postmodern Environment (Wittgensteinian Postmodernism)." In *Sacred Places and Profane Spaces*, ed. J. Scott, 177-190. New York: Greenwood Press, 1991.

**719** Sedmak, Clemens. *Kalkul und Kultur: Studien zu Genesis und Geltung von Wittgensteins Sprachspielmodell.* Amsterdam: Rodopi, 1996.

**720** Sedmak, Clemens. "Wittgensteins Sprachspielmodell und die pluralistische Religionstheorie." *Zeitschrift für Katholische Theologie* 117 (1995): 393-415.

**721** Sellars, Roy Wood. *Reflections on American Philosophy from Within.* Notre Dame: University Notre Dame Press, 1969.

**722** Shah, Anuradha. "Religion, Ethics and Science: A Dialogue between Wittgenstein and Gandhi." *Journal of Indian Council of Philosophical Research* 10 (1993): 27-36.

**723** Shalom, Albert. "A propos d'une publication recente de Wittgenstein." *Dialogue* 6 (1967): 103-113.

**724** Shaw, Jaysankar Lal. "Universal Sentences: Russell, Wittgenstein, Prior, and the Nyaya." *Journal of Indian Philosophy* 19 (1991): 103-119.

**725** Shelley, James Rand. "The Skeptic's Progress: Austin, Wittgenstein, and Contemporary Approaches to Skepticism (J. L. Austin, Robert Nozick, Stanley Cavell)." Ph.D. diss., The University of Chicago, 1995.

**726** Shepherd, John J. "Religion and the Contextualization of Criteria, Part One." *Sophia* 15 (1976): 1-10.

727 Shepherd, William C. "On the Concept of Being Wrong Religiously." *Journal of the American Academy of Religion* 42 (1974): 66-81.

728 Sherry, Patrick. "Is Religion a 'Form of Life'?" *American Philosophical Quarterly* 9 (1972): 159-167.

729 Sherry, Patrick. "Learning How to Be Religious: The Work of Paul Holmer." *Theology* 77 (1974): 81-90.

730 Sherry, Patrick. *Religion, Truth, and Language-Games.* Library of Philosophy and Religion. London: Macmillan, 1977.

731 Sherry, Patrick. "Truth and the 'Religious Language-Game'." *Philosophy* 47 (1972): 18-37.

732 Shibles, Warren. *Death: An Interdisciplinary Analysis.* Whitewater, WI: Language Press, 1974.

733 Shields, George W. "Hartshorne and the Analytic Philosophical Tradition." In *Faith and Creativity*, ed. G. Nordgulen and G. Shields, 197-228. St. Louis, MO: CBP Press, 1987.

734 Shields, Philip R. *Logic and Sin in the Writings of Ludwig Wittgenstein.* Chicago: University of Chicago Press, 1997.

735 Short, Larry Ray. "In a Poetic Fashion: An Inquiry into Language, World, and Religion (Critical Realism, Ordinary Language, Aesthetic Object)." Ph.D. diss., The Florida State University, 1992.

736 Sievert, Donald. "Ethics Does Not Treat of the World — Ethics Must Be a Condition of the World, Like Logic: *Notebooks 1914-1916.*" *Southwest Philosophy Review* 10 (1994): 199-208.

**737** Slater, Peter. "Gastwirth's Concepts of God." *Religious Studies* 9 (1973): 233-235.

**738** Slater, Peter. "Seeing As, Seeing In and Seeing Through." *Sophia* 19 (1980): 10-21.

**739** Smart, R. N. "Death and the Last Judgement." In *Philosophers and Religious Truth*, ed. R. N. Smart. New York: St. Martin's Press, 1969.

**740** Smiley, P. O. "Importance of Wittgenstein." *Tablet* 203 (1954): 116.

**741** Smith, Barry. "Law and Eschatology in Wittgenstein's Early Thought." *Inquiry* 21 (1978): 425-441.

**742** Smith, Huston. "Is Onto-Theology Passé, or Can Religion Endure the Death of Metaphysics." *Religion and Intellectual Life* 3 (1986): 7-14.

**743** Smith, John E. "Faith, Belief, and the Problem of Rationality in Religion." In *Rationality and Religious Belief*, ed. C. Delaney, 42-64. Ann Arbor, Mich.: UMI Books on Demand, 1979.

**744** Smith, John E. *Religion and Empiricism*. Milwaukee: Marquette University Press, 1967.

**745** Smith, P. Christopher. "Gadamer's Hermeneutics and Ordinary Language Philosophy." *Thomist* 43 (1979): 296-321.

**746** Smith-Eivemark, Philip John. "Beyond Language: Mystics and the Language Trap." Ph.D. diss., University of Toronto (Canada), 1996.

**747** Son, Bong Ho. *The Contemporary Spirit and Christian Episte-mology.* Seoul: Sung Kwang, 1978.

**748** Sontag, Frederick. *Wittgenstein and the Mystical: Philosophy as an Ascetic Practice.* American Academy of Religion, Reflection and Theory in the Study of Religion, 2. Atlanta, Ga.: Scholars Press, 1995.

**749** Spaemann, Robert. "Mysticism and Enlightenment." In *The Crisis of Religious Language,* ed. J. B. Metz, 70-83. New York: Herder and Herder, 1973.

**750** Spagnolo, Salvatore. "Genesi e momenti dello 'assoluto realismo' di Vincenzo la Via." *Teoresi* 30 (1975): 209-280.

**751** Spiegelberg, Herbert. "Augustine in Wittgenstein: A Case Study in Philosophical Stimulation." *Journal of the History of Philosophy* (University of California, Berkeley) 17 (1979): 179-196.

**752** Spieler, David A. "Disembodied Existence and the Private Language Argument." *Drew Gateway* 46 (1975-76): 95-105.

**753** Stagaman, David. "'God' in Analytic Philosophy." In *God in Contemporary Thought,* ed. S.A. Matczak, 813-849. New York: Learned Publications, 1977.

**754** Stamey, Joseph D. "Are There Religious Beliefs?" *Southwest Philosophical Studies* 7 (1982): 162-169.

**755** Stanger, James Aaron. "The True Faculty of Knowing: William Blake's Anatomy of the Romantic Body." Ph.D. diss., University of California, Riverside, 1997.

**756** Stashwick, Tad Sergei. "Wittgenstein and Theology: *Philosophi-cal Investigations* Ii, Xi and the Problem of Evil." Ph.D. diss., Yale University, 1983.

**757** Stewart, T. Wesley. "Paul L. Holmer and the Logic of Faith: A Utilization of Kierkegaard and Wittgenstein for Contemporary Christian Theology." Ph.D. diss., The Southern Baptist Theological Seminary, 1991.

**758** Stines, James W. "Language Theory and Hermeneutics in the Thought of Horace Bushnell." *Perspectives in Religious Studies* 7 (1980): 134-150.

**759** Strickler, Nina. "The Problem of the Absolute: a Study in Spinoza, Hegel, and Wittgenstein." Ph.D. diss., DePaul University, 1973.

**760** Strolz, Walter. "Das Problem bei Freud, Wittgenstein und Bloch." In *Der moderne Atheismus; Anstoss zum Christsein,* ed. L. Klein, 23-35. München: J. Pfeiffer, 1970.

**761** Studhalter, Kurt. *Ethik, Religion und Lebensform bei Ludwig Wittgenstein.* Veröffentlichungen der Universität Innsbruck, 82. Innsbruck: Osterr. Kommissionsbuchh. in Komm., 1973.

**762** Surin, Kenneth. "The Trinity and Philosophical Reflections: A Study of David Brown's *The Divine Trinity." Modern Theology* 2 (1986): 235-256.

**763** Sutherland, Stewart R. "On the Idea of a Form of Life." *Religious Studies* 11 (1975): 293-306.

**764** Swatos, William H. "Liturgy and Lebensform: The Personal God as a Social Being." *Perspectives in Religious Studies* 7 (1980): 38-49.

765  Tabor, Fred Matthew. "A Critique of Wittgenstein's Impact on the Contemporary Philosophy of Religion." Thesis (M.S.), University of Utah, Department of Philosophy, 1983.

766  Tarbox, Everett J., Jr. "Linguistic Pragmatism: William James and Ludwig Wittgenstein." *American Journal of Theology and Philosophy* 15 (1994): 43-58.

767  Tarbox, Everett J., Jr. "The Possibilities of Religious Language: A Dialogue between Gordon Kaufman and Ludwig Wittgenstein." In *New Essays in Religious Pluralism*, ed. L. Axel, 235-246. Macon, Ga: Mercer University Press, 1993.

768  Tarbox, Everett J., Jr. "Wittgenstein, James and a Bridge to Radical Empiricism." *American Journal of Theology and Philosophy* 13 (1992): 89-103.

769  Tavard, George H. "Sexist Language in Theology?" *Theological Studies* 36 (1975): 700-724.

770  Tessin, Timothy, and Mario von der Ruhr, eds. *Philosophy and the Grammar of Religious Belief (Papers from a Conference Held at the Claremont Graduate School)*, Claremont Studies in the Philosophy of Religion. New York: St. Martin's Press, 1995.

771  Theron, D. S. "Morality as Right Reason." *Monist* 66 (1983): 26-38.

772  Thiselton, Anthony C. *Interpreting God and the Postmodern Self: On Meaning, Manipulation and Promise*. Grand Rapids: Eerdmans, 1995.

773  Thiselton, Anthony C. "Knowledge, Myth and Corporate Memory." In *Believing in the Church*, ed. B. Mitchell, 45-78. London: SPCK, 1981.

**774**  Thiselton, Anthony C. "Meaning of *Sarx* in 1 Corinthians 5:5: A Fresh Approach in the Light of Logical and Semantic Factors." *Scottish Journal of Theology* 26 (1973): 204-228.

**775**  Thiselton, Anthony C. *New Horizons in Hermeneutics: The Theory and Practice of Transforming Biblical Reading.* Grand Rapids: Zondervan, 1992.

**776**  Thiselton, Anthony C. "The Parables as Language-Event: Some Comments on Fuchs's Hermeneutics in the Light of Linguistic Philosophy." *Scottish Journal of Theology* 23 (1970): 437-468.

**777**  Thiselton, Anthony C. "The Supposed Power of Words in the Biblical Writings." *Journal of Theological Studies* 25 (1974): 283-299.

**778**  Thiselton, Anthony C. *The Two Horizons: New Testament Hermeneutics and Philosophical Description.* Grand Rapids: Eerdmans, 1980.

**779**  Thistlethwaite, Susan Brooks. "Inclusive Language: Theological and Philosophical Fragments." *Religious Education* 80 (1985): 551-570.

**780**  Thomas, E. Vaughan. "Wittgenstein and Tolstoy: The Authentic Orientation." *Religious Studies: An International Journal for the Philosophy of Religion* 33 (1997): 363-377.

**781**  Thomas, E. Vaughan. "Wittgensteinian Methodology and Religious Belief." *International Philosophical Quarterly* 39 (1999): 265-275.

**782**  Thomas, E. Vaughan. "Wittgensteinian Perspectives *Sub Specie Aeternitatis.*" *Religious Studies* 31 (1995): 329-340.

**783** Thompson, Caleb. "Wittgenstein's Confessions: A Study of the Influence of Augustine's and Tolstoy's Confessions on the Philosophy of Wittgenstein (Ludwig Wittgenstein, Saint Augustine, Leo Tolstoy)." Ph.D. diss., University of Virginia, 1994.

**784** Thornton, Stephen P. "Facing Up to Feuerbach." *International Journal for Philosophy of Religion* 39 (1996): 103-120.

**785** Thornton, Stephen P. "Sempiternity, Immortality and the Homunculus Fallacy." *Philosophical Investigations* 16 (1993): 307-326.

**786** Tilghman, B. R. "Isn't Belief in God an Attitude." *International Journal for Philosophy of Religion* 43 (1998): 17-28.

**787** Tilghman, B. R. *Wittgenstein, Ethics and Aesthetics: The View from Eternity.* SUNY Series in Ethical Theory. Albany: State University of New York Press, 1991.

**788** Todisco, Orlando. "Il doppio volto dell'ineffabile in L Wittgenstein." *Sapienza* (1991): 13-24.

**789** Tominaga, Thomas T. "Taoist and Wittgensteinian Mysticism." *Journal of Chinese Philosophy* 9 (1982): 269-289.

**790** Tominaga, Thomas T. "A Wittgensteinian Analysis of the Depth Grammar of Religious Belief and Practice." In *Philosophy of Religion*, ed. W. Gombocz, 183-186. Vienna: Hölder-Pichler-Tempsky, 1984.

**791** Topping, Richard R. "Transcendental Method and Private Language (Language and Experience in Lonergan and Wittgenstein)." *Arc (0229-2807)* 21 (1993): 11-26.

792  Tornos, Andrés. "Experiencia, lógica y lenguaje en las filosofías de la religión: dos lecturas de Wittgenstein." *Miscelanea Comillas* 47 (1989): 391-413.

793  Tornos, Andres. "La filosofia del cristianismo y de la religion en Wittgenstein." *Pensamiento* 46 (1990): 23-47.

794  Trethowan, I. "Importance of Wittgenstein." *Tablet* 203 (1954): 140.

795  Trundle, Robert. "St. Thomas and Modal Logic: On Wittgenstein's and Heidegger's 'Possibility'." *Aquinas* 38 (1995): 223-248.

796  Trundle, Robert. "St. Thomas' Modal Logic: Did Wittgenstein and Heidegger Embrace It?" *Idealist Studies: An Interdisciplinary Journal of Philosophy* 26 (1996): 79-99.

797  Trundle, Robert. "St. Thomas on Wittgenstein and Heidegger: The World's Possible Nonexistence." *Giornale di Metafisica* 17 (1995): 327-360.

798  Työrinoja, Reijo J. "Private Language and Religious Experience." In *Philosophy of Religion*, ed. W. Gombocz, 167-169. Vienna: Hölder-Pichler-Tempsky, 1984.

799  Työrinoja, Reijo J. "Wittgenstein and Postmodernism." In *Philosophical Studies in Religion, Metaphysics, and Ethics*, ed. Timo Koistinen and Tommi Lehtonen, 160-178. Helsinki: Luther-Agricola-Society, 1997.

800  Upper, John K. "Wittgenstein and Peirce (Ludwig Wittgenstein, Charles S. Peirce)." M.A. thesis, Queen's University at Kingston (Canada), 1992.

**801**  Van Buren, Paul. *The Edges of Language: An Essay in the Logic of Religion.* New York: Macmillan, 1972.

**802**  Van Buren, Paul. "Reply to J.P. Carse." *Theology Today* 24 (1967): 227-229.

**803**  Van Buren, Paul. *The Secular Meaning of the Gospel.* New York: Macmillan, 1963.

**804**  Van Woudenberg, Rene. "Theistic Arguments and the Crisis of Classical Foundationalism (in Dutch)." *Bijdragen, Tijdschrift voor Filosofie en Theologie* 58 (1997): 2-28.

**805**  Vanhoozer, Kevin J. "The Semantics of Biblical Literature: Truth and Scripture's Diverse Literary Forms." In *Hermeneutics, Authority, and Canon*, ed. D. Carson and J. Woodbridge, 53-104. Grand Rapids: Academic Books, 1986.

**806**  Vargas, Alberto. "Etica sin raices." *Dianoia* (1989): 117-122.

**807**  Vasa, Andrea. "L'ateismo religioso di L Wittgenstein." In *Esistenza, mito, ermeneutica: scritti per Enrico Castelli*, ed. M. Olivetti, 285-313. Padova: CEDAM, 1980.

**808**  Verbin, Nehama. "The Mystical Element in Wittgenstein's *Tractatus*: The Relation Between the Logical and the Mystical (Ludwig Wittgenstein)." M.A. thesis, University of St. Michael's College (Canada), 1996.

**809**  Vergote, A.Bultmann; . "Verticaliteit En Horizontaliteit In Het Symbolische Spreken Over God." *Tijdschrft voor Filosofie* 31 (1969): 638-669.

**810**  Vincent, Gilbert. "Le sujet de la croyance langage, croyance et institution." *Revue d'histoire et de philosophie religieuses* 65 (1985): 271-295.

**811**  Visvader, John. "The Use of Paradox in Uroboric Philosophies." *Philosophy East and West* 28 (1978): 455-467.

**812**  Viswanathan, K. S. "Existence after the God-Man: Kierkegaard, Wittgenstein, and the Paradox of Christian Youth." Ph.D. diss., University of Essex, 1996.

**813**  von Der Ruhr, Mario Peter Walter. "Ritual and Religion: Responses to Positivism (Vienna Circle, Ludwig Wittgenstein)." Ph.D. diss., University of Illinois at Urbana-Champaign, 1996.

**814**  Vree, Dale. "Reflections on Wittgenstein, Religion, and Politics." *Christian Scholar's Review* 3 (1973): 113-133.

**815**  Wabel, Thomas. *Sprache als Grenze: in Luthers theologischer Hermeneutik und Wittgensteins Sprachphilosophie.* Hawthorne: de-Gruyter, 1998.

**816**  Wahlström, Bertel. "The Relativity of Meaning (Critique of J. Skorupsi's Relativist Approach to Social Beliefs, Traditions." *Religious Studies* 22 (1986): 205-217.

**817**  Waismann, Friedrich. *Ludwig Wittgenstein and the Vienna Circle.* New York: Barnes & Noble, 1979.

**818**  Waismann, Friedrich. "Notes on Talks with Wittgenstein." *The Philosophical Review* 74 (1965): 12-16.

**819**  Wallace, Raymond P. "A Consideration of Wittgenstein's Use of 'Gewissheit' and 'Sicherheit' (in *On Certainty*)." In

*Tradition as Openness to the Future: Essays in Honor of Willis W. Fisher,* ed. F. Francis and R. Wallace, 199-216. Lanham, MD: University Press of America, 1984.

**820** Walsh, Brian J.Bultmann;. "Anthony Thiselton's Contribution to Biblical Hermeneutics." *Christian Scholar's Review* 14 (1985): 224-235.

**821** Watt, A. J. "Religious Beliefs and Pictures." *Sophia* 9 (1970): 1-7.

**822** Weeks, Andrew. *German Mysticism from Hildegard of Bingen to Ludwig Wittgenstein: A Literary and Intellectual History.* Albany: State University of New York Press, 1993.

**823** Weger, Karl-Heinz. *Religionskritik von der Aufklärung bis zur Gegenwart: Autoren-Lexikon von Adorno bis Wittgenstein.* 3 Aufl. ed. Herderbucherei, 716. Freiburg im Breisgau: Herder, 1983.

**824** Wellmer, A. "Empirico-Analytical and Critical Social Science." *Continuum* 8 (1970-1971): 12-26.

**825** Wenderoth, Christine. "Otto's View on Language: The Evidence of *Das Heilige.*" *Perspectives in Religious Studies* 9 (1982): 39-48.

**826** West, Cornel. "Schleiermacher's Hermeneutics and the Myth of the Given." *Union Seminary Quarterly Review* 34 (1979): 71-84.

**827** Westergaard, Peter K. "Mennesket—et ceremonielt dyr: L Wittgensteins *Bemerkungen über Frazers Golden Bough.*" *Dansk Teologisk Tidsskrift* 56 (1993): 280-303.

**828**  Westergaard, Peter K. "'...Predestination in St Paul, is...': Wittgenstein's Religious-Philosophical Notes of August-December 1937." In *Arbeiten zu Wittgenstein*, ed. H Wilhelm Kruger. Bergen: Wittgenstein-Arch, 1998.

**829**  Westphal, Jonathan, ed. *Certainty.* Indianapolis: Hackett, 1995.

**830**  White, Harvey W. "God and Philosophical Grammar." *Philosophical Studies (Ireland)* 30 (1984): 177-181.

**831**  White, Roger. "Notes on Analogical Predication and Speaking about God." In *Philosophical Frontiers of Christian Theology: Essays Presented to D. MacKinnon*, ed. B. Hebblethwaite, 197-226. New York: Cambridge University Press, 1982.

**832**  White, Roger. "Riddles and Anselm's Riddle." *The Aristotelian Society: Supplementary Volume* 51 (1977): 169-186.

**833**  Whittaker, John. "Christianity is Not a Doctrine." In *The Grammar of the Heart: New Essays in Moral Philosophy and Theology*, ed. R. Bell, 54-74. San Francisco: Harper and Row, 1988.

**834**  Whittaker, John. "'Forms of Life' and Religious Belief." Ph.D. diss., Yale University, 1974.

**835**  Whittaker, John. "Language Games and Forms of Life Unconfused." *Philosophical Investigations* 1 (1978): 39-48.

**836**  Whittaker, John. *Matters of Faith and Matters of Principle: Religious Truth Claims and Their Logic.* San Antonio: Trinity University Press, 1981.

**837** Whittaker, John. *"Tractatus* 64312: Immortality and the Riddle of Life." *Philosophical Investigations* 6 (1983): 37-48.

**838** Whittaker, John. "Wittgenstein and Religion: Some Later Views of his Later Work." *Religious Studies Review* 4 (1978): 188-193.

**839** Wienpahl, Paul. "Eastern Buddhism and Wittgenstein's *Philosophical Investigations.*" *Eastern Buddhist* 12 (1979): 22-54.

**840** Williams, Rowan. "The Suspicion of Suspicion: Wittgenstein and Bonhoeffer." In *The Grammar of the Heart: New Essays in Moral Philosophy and Theology,* ed. R. Bell, 36-53. San Francisco: Harper and Row, 1988.

**841** Wilson, Ivan Benjamin Uriah. "The Concept of Religious Belief (Beliefs)." Ph.D. diss., University of Exeter (United Kingdom), 1991.

**842** Wilson, Kenneth. *Making Sense of It: An Essay in Philosophical Theology.* London: Epworth Press, 1973.

**843** Wimmer, Reiner. "Wittgensteins Wiederholung der Einsicht Kierkegaards in die Paradoxalität des Begriffs des Ethischen und des Religiösen." In *Philosophy of Religion: International Wittgenstein Symposium 1983,* ed. W. Gombocz, 187-189. Vienna: Hölder-Pichler-Tempsky, 1984.

**844** Winch, Peter. "Darwin Und Die Genesis—Ein Widerspruch: Fragen Zur Religionsphilosophie." *Conceptus: Zeitschrift für Philosophie* 15 (1981): 37-42.

**845** Winch, Peter. "Language, Belief and Relativism." In *Contemporary British Philosophy: Personal Statements,* ed. Hywel David Lewis. London: George Allen and Unwin, 1976.

846 Winch, Peter. "Picture and Representation." In *Trying to Make Sense*, ed. Peter Winch, 64-80. Oxford: Blackwell, 1987.

847 Winch, Peter. *Simone Weil: 'The Just Balance'.* Cambridge: Cambridge University Press, 1989.

848 Winch, Peter. *Trying to Make Sense.* Oxford: Blackwell, 1987.

849 Winch, Peter. "Understanding a Primitive Society." *American Philosophical Quarterly* 1 (1964): 307-324.

850 Wisdo, David. "Kierkegaard and Euthyphro." *Philosophy* 62 (1987): 221-226.

851 Wisdom, John. "Gods." *Proceedings of the Aristotelian Society* 45 (1944-45): 185-206.

852 Wisdom, John. *Paradox and Discovery.* Oxford: Basil Blackwell, 1965.

853 Wisdom, John. *Philosophy and Psychoanalysis.* Oxford: Basil Blackwell, 1953.

854 Witherspoon, Edward Newell Jr. "Nonsense, Logic, and Skepticism (Rudolph Carnap, Ludwig Wittgenstein, Martin Heidegger, Friedrich Frege, Epistemology)." Ph.D. diss., University of Pittsburgh, 1996.

855 Woelfel, James W. "Will Wittgenstein Experience the Last Judgment?" *Encounter* 40 (1979): 49-61.

856 Wohlman, Avital. "Michel Serres (in Hebrew)." *Iyyun* 45 (1996): 443-460.

857  Wood, Charles. *The Formation of Christian Understanding*. Philadelphia: Westminster, 1981.

858  Wren, David John. "Privacy and the Language of Faith." Ph.D. diss., Yale University, 1973.

859  Wright, G. H. von. "Wittgenstein in Relation to His Times." In *Wittgenstein and His Times*, ed. B. McGuinness, 108-120. Chicago: University of Chicago Press, 1982.

860  Wuchterl, Kurt. "Religionsphilosophie nach Wittgenstein." In *Philosophy of Religion: International Wittgenstein Symposium 1983*, ed. W. Gombocz, 60-62. Vienna: Hölder-Pichler-Tempsky, 1984.

861  Wuchterl, Kurt. "Thesen zur analytischen Religions philosophie." *Philosophisches Jahrbuch* 88 (1981): 343-356.

862  Xirau, Ramon. *Cuatro filosofos y lo sagrado: Teilhard de Chardin, Heidegger, Wittgenstein, Simone Weil.* Cuadernos de Joaquin Mortiz. Mexico, D.F.: Editorial Joaquin Mortiz, 1986.

863  Xirau, Ramon. "Presencia De Limite: Wittgenstein Y 'Lo Mistico'." *Dianoia* 28 (1982): 261-274.

864  Yin, Lu-Jun. "Against Destiny: Feng Yu-Lan and a New Hermeneutics of Confucianism (China)." Ph.D. diss., Stanford University, 1992.

865  Yong, Huang. "Foundation of Religious Beliefs after Foundationalism: Wittgenstein between Nielsen and Phillips." *Religious Studies* 31 (1995): 251-267.

866  York, Anne. "Wittgenstein's Later Mysticism." *Theology* 100 (1997): 352-363.

**867** Young, Julian. "Wittgenstein, Kant, Schopenhauer, and Critical Philosophy." *Theoria* 50 (1984): 73-105.

**868** Young, William. "Wittgenstein and Christianity." In *Philosophy of Religion*, ed. W. Gambocz, 153-156, 1984.

**869** Young, William. "Wittgenstein and Predestination." In *Wittgenstein and His Impact on Contemporary Thought*, ed. E. Leinfellner, 513-516. Vienna: Hölder-Pichler-Tempsky, 1978.

**870** Young, William. "Wittgenstein and the Future of Metaphysics." In *The Tasks Of Contemporary Philosophy*, ed. Werner Leinfellner, 291-293. Vienna: Hölder-Pichler-Tempsky, 1986.

**871** Zeis, John. "Wittgenstein: Kritik and the Problem of Religious Language." M.A. thesis, Niagara University, 1976.

**872** Zemach, Eddy. "Wittgenstein's Philosophy of the Mystical." *The Review of Metaphysics* 18 (1964): 38-57.

**873** Zorn, Hans. "Grammar, Doctrines, and Practice: Lindbeck's 'Cultural-linguistic' Analysis of Religion and Doctrine." *Journal of Religion* 75 (1995): 509-520.

**874** Zuurdeeg, W.F. "Implications of Analytical Philosophy for Theology." *Journal of Bible and Religion* 29 (1961): 204-210.

# SUBJECT INDEX

Aesthetics

Analytic philosophy

Anselm

Anthropology

Aquinas, Thomas

[Barrett, 1992 #39; Beardsley, 1974 #50; Bruening, 1977 #93; Burrows, 1993 #111; Clarke, 1967 #158; Daly, 1961 #196; Edwards, 1972 #235; Fortuna, 1989 #261; Garceau, 1975 #267; Gutting, 1982 #323; Hawkins, 1957 #346; Hill, 1987 #369; Hudson, 1974 #391; Inciarte, 1975 #410; Kenny, 1959 #448; King-Farlow, 1984 #457; McCabe, 1992 #525; Newport, 1985 #569; O'Callaghan, 1996 #599; Pouivet, 1997 #655; Rotella, 1975 #694; Sellars, 1969 #721; Trundle, 1995 #795; Trundle, 1995 #797; Trundle, 1996 #796; van Woudenberg, 1997 #804; Waismann, 1979 #817; White, 1982 #831]

Arianism

[Norris, 1993 #593]

Aristotle

[Inciarte, 1975 #410; Lear, 1984 #481; Miller, 1973 #546; Waismann, 1979 #817]

Art

[Bell, 1986 #56; Gill, 1975 #288; Gill, 1978 #283; Rhees, 1969 #682]

Atheism

[Brümmer, 1994 #96; Charlesworth, 1970 #135; Garceau, 1975 #267; Henderson, 1979 #354; Hubík, 1984 #385; Ladrière, 1970 #469; Nielsen, 1989 #580; Phillips, 1970 #644; Sarot, 1993 #703; van Buren, 1972 #801; van Woudenberg, 1997 #804; Vasa, 1980 #807]

Augustine, Saint

[Ayers, 1976 #28; Baum, 1980 #46; Burnyeat, 1999 #107; Eastmen, 1969 #231; Embree, 1991 #239; McNulty, 1975 #539; Spiegelberg, 1979 #751; Thompson, 1994 #783; Waismann, 1979 #817]

Austin, John

[Arens, 1985 #22; Bahnsen, 1976 #29; Holmes, 1969 #381; Larson, 1978 #473; Luijpen, 1973 #497; Magee, 1971 #504; Shelley, 1995 #725; Vanhoozer, 1986 #805]

Ayer, Alfred Jules

[Blackstone, 1963 #68; Heimbeck, 1969 #350; Laura, 1972 #478; Luijpen, 1973 #497; Magee, 1971 #504; Thiselton, 1992 #775]

Barbour, Ian

[D'Costa, 1985 #205; Gutting, 1982 #323]

Barth, Karl

[Brecher, 1983 #81; Bretall, 1987 #86; Brümmer, 1994 #98; Fairley, 1991 #248; Helme, 1981 #352; Krieg, 1997 #462; Madden, 1967 #501; Maurer, 1990 #524; Morse, 1982 #558; White, 1982 #831]

Belief, religious

[Balmuth, 1984 #31; Banner, 1986 #36; Bar-Elli, 1993 #37; Barrett, 1991 #40; Barrett, 1994 #38; Bearn, 1984 #51; Beckman, 1990 #53; Blackstone, 1963 #68; Braithwaite, 1955 #78; Browarzik, 1988 #90; Burke, 1978 #105; Chandra, 1997 #133; Christian, 1981 #141; Churchill, 1981 #151; Churchill, 1984 #149;

Berger, Peter

[Swatos, 1980 #764]

Bible

[Bruce, 1988 #92; Cruickshank, 1970 #190; Eller, 1982 #237; Feinberg, 1978 #250; Geisler, 1977 #276; Geisler, 1978 #277; Gruenler, 1981 #315; Hellerer, 1984 #351; Jasper, 1985 #417; Kellenberger, 1990 #443; Kelsey, 1975 #446; Kelsey, 1980 #447; Maurer, 1990 #524; Mondin, 1993 #550; Nielsen, 1976 #576; Porter, 1989 #652; Scobel, 1981 #717; Thiselton, 1970 #776; Thiselton, 1973 #774; Thiselton, 1974 #777; Thiselton, 1992 #775; Thiselton, 1995 #772; van Buren, 1963 #803; Vanhoozer, 1986 #805; Walsh, 1985 #820; Westergaard, 1998 #828; Winch, 1981 #844; Young, 1984 #868]

Blake, William

[Stanger, 1997 #755]

Body

[Gill, 1982 #292; Gillett, 1985 #294; Grünfeld, 1975 #317; Thiselton, 1973 #774]

Bonaventure

[Crosson, 1981 #189]

Bonhoeffer, Dietrich

[Williams, 1988 #840]

Bouwsma, O.K.

[Craft, 1984 #184; Hustwit, 1992 #406; Jones, 1971 #425]

Buber, Martin

[Caine, 1993 #113]

Buddhism

[Boero-Vargas, 1998 #71; Bugault, 1990 #99; Bugault, 1986 #100; D'Costa, 1985 #205; Della Santina, 1986 #208; Garner, 1977 #268; Gudmunsen, 1974 #319; Gudmunsen, 1977 #320; Hudson, 1973 #397; Kalansuriya, 1977 #431; Kalansuriya, 1987 #430; Kalupahana, 1977 #432; Katz, 1977 #434; Kurosaki, 1987 #465; Martin, 1988 #518; McLean, 1986 #538; Richards, 1978 #684; Visvader, 1978 #811; Wienpahl, 1979 #839]

Bultmann, Rudolf

[Macquarrie, 1967 #500; Martin, 1978 #514; Thiselton, 1980 #778; Thiselton, 1992 #775; Walsh, 1985 #820]

Bunyan, John

[Baum, 1980 #46]

Catholicism

[Coulson, 1958 #179; Cranston, 1951 #185; Davies, 1984 #200; Kerr, 1999 #454; Smiley, 1954 #740; Trethowan, 1954 #794]

Cavell, Stanley

[Bearn, 1984 #51; Brown, 1986 #91; Cavell, 1996 #130; Hustwit, 1978 #407; Irwin, 1995 #413; Shelley, 1995 #725]

Certainty

[Allen, 1972 #4; Armengaud, 1983 #23; Ayer, 1985 #27; Beardsley, 1974 #50; Bearn, 1984 #51; Browarzik, 1988 #90; Churchland, 1987 #154; Gill, 1974 #287; High, 1981 #366; High, 1986 #365; Ho, 1991 #370; Kaufman, 1999 #435; Kellenberger, 1972 #441; Langworthy, 1984 #471; Martin, 1984 #517; McCarthy, 1982 #526; Moen, 1979 #547; Robinson, 1976 #690; Shields, 1997 #734; Wallace, 1984 #819; Westphal, 1995 #829; Whittaker, 1981 #836]

Chomsky, Noam

[Hudson, 1981 #393; Nicolet, 1989 #571]

Christendom

[Cameron, 1981 #115]

Christology

[Carse, 1967 #125; Crosson, 1981 #189; Devenish, 1983 #209; Gruenler, 1981 #315]

Coleridge, Samuel Taylor

[Priestley, 1982 #663]

Confucianism

[Patt-Shamir, 1997 #616]

Conversion

[Dilman, 1975 #217; Raschke, 1978 #676]

Cosmology

[Miller, 1986 #545]

Creation

[Bruening, 1982 #94]

Cross cultural comparison

[Bell, 1978 #61; Dov Lerner, 1995 #222; Johnstone, 1993 #424; Kellenberger, 1983 #442; Kowal, 1994 #461; Lillegard, 1984 #489; Rhees, 1982 #683]

*Culture and Value*

[Burke, 1994 #103; Holland, 1990 #374; Puelles, 1993 #666]

Davidson, Donald

[Caine, 1993 #113]

de Chardin, Teillard

[Xirau, 1986 #862]

Death

[Kroy, 1982 #463; Phillips, 1970 #629; Shibles, 1974 #732; Smart, 1969 #739; Thornton, 1993 #785]

Deconstruction

[Edwards, 1989 #232; Garner, 1985 #269; Ruf, 1989 #698]

Derrida, Jacques

[Embree, 1991 #239; Magnus, 1995 #507; Ruf, 1989 #698; Smith, 1986 #742; Thiselton, 1992 #775; West, 1979 #826]

Descartes, Rene

[Bugault, 1986 #100; Edwards, 1982 #233; Farrelly, 1973 #249; Gillett, 1985 #294; Haller, 1989 #330; McGhee, 1996 #531; Moran, 1997 #556; Waismann, 1979 #817; Wallace, 1984 #819]

Dewey, John

[Bahnsen, 1976 #29]

Dialectical theology

[Baltazar, 1981 #32]

Doctrine

[Bambrough, 1991 #34; Emmanuel, 1989 #240; Hallett, 1975 #331; Harrison, 1964 #341; Lindbeck, 1984 #490; Putti, 1982 #670; Whittaker, 1988 #833]

Dogma, see: Doctrine

Dostoyevsky, Fyodor

[Baum, 1980 #46]

Doubt, see: Skepticism

Dummett, Michael

[Beards, 1995 #49]

Ecology

[Burkhardt, 1983 #106]

Education, philosophy of

[Beehler, 1978 #54; Fiorenza, 1987 #257; Hustwit, 1992 #406; Jager, 1972 #415; Martin, 1987 #516; McLaughlin, 1995 #537; Poupore, 1993 #658; Priestley, 1982 #663]

Empiricism

[Antiseri, 1975 #15; Braithwaite, 1955 #78; Dilley, 1976 #215; Grünfeld, 1983 #316; Lazerowitz, 1976 #480; Richmond, 1970 #686; Smith, 1967 #744; Tarbox, 1992 #768; Wellmer, 1970-1971 #824]

Emptiness

[Cheng, 1981 #139; Della Santina, 1986 #208; McLean, 1986 #538; Ryder, 1982 #700; Schroeder, 1996 #714]

Epistemology

[Allen, 1972 #4; Bahnsen, 1976 #29; Bearn, 1984 #51; Bearn, 1993 #52; Bell, 1995 #58; Blackstone, 1963 #68; Brent, 1982 #85; Caine, 1993 #113; Campana, 1989 #116; Canfield, 1993 #120; Christian, 1981 #141; Churchill, 1987 #142; Churchland, 1987 #154; Curnutt, 1998 #192; Davis, 1984 #204; Geisler, 1977 #276; Gill, 1969 #290; Gill, 1975 #288; Gill, 1981 #282; Gill, 1982 #292; Grant, 1995 #308; Grim, 1988 #314; Grünfeld, 1975 #317; Grünfeld, 1983 #316; Hallett, 1977 #333; Harrison, 1988 #342; Lerner, 1994 #486; Miller, 1973 #546; Murphy, 1995 #562; Otubanjo, 1979 #607; Patterson, 1991 #615; Patterson, 1992 #614; Penco, 1989 #619; Peregrin, 1993 #621; Saunders, 1976 #705; Schmidt, 1985 #712; Sedmak, 1996 #719; Son, 1978 #747;

Thornton, 1993 #785; Tilghman, 1998 #786; Trundle, 1996 #796; Whittaker, 1988 #833; Witherspoon, 1996 #854]

Eschatology

[Baltazar, 1981 #32; Krieg, 1997 #462; Kroy, 1982 #463; Ray, 1990 #679; Smith, 1978 #741]

Esotericism

[Anderson, 1990 #12]

Essentialism

[Anderson, 1990 #12]

Eternity

[Arnswald, 1998 #26]

Ethics

[Abramson, 1987 #1; Arnswald, 1998 #26; Baldini, 1993 #30; Barrett, 1991 #40; Barrett, 1994 #38; Bassols, 1989 #43; Beehler, 1978 #54; Berenson, 1984 #64; Brenner, 1991 #82; Britton, 1962 #88; Brose, 1994 #89; Burkhardt, 1983 #106; Campana, 1989 #116; Canfield, 1986 #118; Cox, 1976 #182; Creegan, 1989 #187; Daly, 1956 #194; Dragona-Monachou, 1980 #226; Edwards, 1982 #233; Elstein, 1991 #238; Embree, 1991 #239; Frongia, 1971 #263; Gaita, 1990 #265; Gehl, 1986 #275; Hurley, 1985 #402; Hustwit, 1985 #404; Indiana, 1985 #411; Jarrett, 1994 #416; Jespers, 1998 #418; Jones, 1975 #427; Kaufman, 1999 #435; Lear, 1984 #481; Leier, 1994 #483; Loades, 1981 #493; Maesschalck, 1990 #503; Maesschalck, 1991 #502; Marini, 1989 #509; Martin, 1972 #512; McDonald, 1986 #529; McFarlane, 1996 #530; McLaughlin, 1987 #536; O'Connor, 1996 #600; Pellecchia, 1994

Evil

Existentialism

Experience, religious, see: Religious experience

Faith

Langworthy, 1984 #471; Loades, 1981 #493; Luijpen, 1973 #497; MacIntyre, 1970 #499; Martin, 1978 #514; Martin, 1984 #517; Miller, 1983 #544; Moen, 1979 #547; Morse, 1982 #558; Nielsen, 1982 #589; Ommen, 1980 #605; Ott, 1971 #606; Phillips, 1970 #632; Phillips, 1988 #631; Pititto, 1997 #647; Porter, 1989 #652; Portmann, 1986 #654; Poulain, 1970 #656; Putnam, 1991 #669; Roberts, 1986 #688; Rowe, 1989 #695; Rudebush, 1979 #696; Shepherd, 1974 #727; Smith, 1979 #743; Stewart, 1991 #757; Thiselton, 1981 #773; Thomas, 1995 #782; Tornos, 1990 #793; Vincent, 1985 #810; Waismann, 1979 #817; Westphal, 1995 #829; Whittaker, 1981 #836; Wren, 1973 #858]

Falsification

[Armengaud, 1983 #23; Campbell, 1971 #117; Casper, 1972 #127; Charlesworth, 1961 #136; Churchland, 1987 #154; Feinberg, 1978 #250; Garceau, 1975 #267; Greisch, 1991 #310; Heimbeck, 1969 #350; High, 1972 #362; Kjärgaard, 1982 #459; Liverziani, 1971 #492; Luijpen, 1973 #497; Martin, 1984 #517; Nielsen, 1973 #586; Phillips, 1965 #628; Purtill, 1975 #668]

Family resemblance

[Brent, 1982 #85; Downing, 1972 #225; McDermott, 1970 #528; Midgley, 1974 #542; Slater, 1973 #737]

Feminism

[Churchill, 1994 #153; Eller, 1982 #237; Lee-Lampshire, 1991 #482; Rudy, 1993 #697; Tavard, 1975 #769; Thistlethwaite, 1985 #779]

Feuerbach, Ludwig

[Thornton, 1996 #784]

Feyerabend, Paul

[Davis, 1984 #204]

Fideism

[Bell, 1995 #58; Bildhauer, 1972 #66; Cameron, 1981 #115; Dilley, 1976 #215; Downing, 1972 #225; Hall, 1979 #329; High, 1967 #363; Huang, 1995 #384; Hudson, 1968 #390; Hudson, 1970 #398; Keeling, 1977 #437; Nielsen, 1967 #588; Nielsen, 1969 #590; Nielsen, 1972 #578; Nielsen, 1982 #589; Ommen, 1980 #605; Penelhum, 1986 #620; Ralls, 1996 #673; Rowe, 1989 #695; Shepherd, 1976 #726]

Form of life

[Bar-Elli, 1993 #37; Barrie, 1980 #41; Brent, 1982 #85; Cameron, 1981 #115; Creegan, 1989 #187; Curnutt, 1998 #192; Drob, 1988 #228; Hamilton, 1979 #336; High, 1967 #363; Hustwit, 1978 #407; Kasachkoff, 1970 #433; Magnanini, 1979 #506; Martin, 1981 #519; Nielsen, 1975-1976 #585; O'Keeffe, 1980 #603; Phillips, 1981 #627; Phillips, 1986 #626; Quinn, 1976 #671; Raschke, 1974 #674; Ray, 1988 #678; Ray, 1990 #677; Shalom, 1967 #723; Shepherd, 1976 #726; Sherry, 1972 #728; Studhalter, 1973 #761; Sutherland, 1975 #763; Swatos, 1980 #764; Whittaker, 1974 #834; Whittaker, 1978 #835]

Foundationalism

[Curnutt, 1998 #192; Guarino, 1995 #318; High, 1981 #366; Huang, 1995 #384; Nielsen, 1986 #583; Phillips, 1976 #637; Phillips, 1981 #643; Phillips, 1988 #631; van Woudenberg, 1997 #804; Yong, 1995 #865]

Frazer's *The Golden Bough*, see: *Golden Bough*

Frege, Gottlob

Freud, Sigmund

Gadamer, Hans-Georg

God talk

God, concept of

Nebreda, 1994 #564; Nielsen, 1972 #574; Nielsen, 1980 #587; Nielsen, 1987 #579; Nuechterlien, 1995 #595; Slater, 1973 #737; Smith, 1967 #744; Stagaman, 1977 #753; Thiselton, 1995 #772; White, 1984 #830; Wisdom, John, 1944-45 #851]

God, existence of

[Heaney, 1980 #349; Henderson, 1979 #354; Hopkins, 1978 #382; Kasachkoff, 1970 #433; Kellenberger, 1972 #441; Magnus, 1995 #507; Moore, 1988 #552; Nielsen, 1980 #587; Nielsen, 1984 #582; Nielsen, 1987 #579; Nielsen, 1989 #580]

God, knowableness

[Barrett, 1992 #39; Cell, 1978 #131; Disbrey, 1994 #220; Hill, 1987 #369; Lash, 1988 #474; Martin, 1981 #519; Power, 1976 #660; Westphal, 1995 #829; White, 1982 #831]

God, language of

[Bruening, 1977 #93; Burrows, 1993 #111; Charlesworth, 1961 #136; Gill, 1968 #280; Harrison, 1964 #341; Hesse, 1969 #361; Leuze, 1984 #487; Macquarrie, 1967 #500; Mondin, 1993 #550; Schedler, 1974 #710; Schweizer-Bjelic, 1990 #716; Vergote, 1969 #809]

Golden Bough

[Bell, 1978 #61; Bouveresse, 1993 #75; Churchill, 1992 #144; Clack, 1996 #156; Collins, 1996 #165; Davies,1983 #203; Hudson, 1981 #387; O'Hear, 1978 #601; Phillips, 1986 #635; Rhees, 1982 #683; Sachs, 1988 #701; Westergaard, 1993 #827; Winch, 1964 #849]

Grammar, religious

[Bassols, 1989 #43; Bell, 1968 #60; Bell, 1969 #62; Bell, 1975 #59; Bhat, 1996 #65; Brenner, 1996 #83; Burrell, 1970 #110; Carlson, 1983 #122; Churchill, 1981 #151; Churchill, 1995 #145]

Habermas, Jürgen

[Arens, 1985 #22]

Hegel, Georg Wihelm Friedrich

[Cook, 1987 #168; Hustwit, 1992 #406; Lear, 1984 #481; Miller, 1973 #546; Strickler, 1973 #759; Waismann, 1979 #817]

Heidegger, Martin

[Bindeman, 1978 #67; Bourbon, 1996 #72; Edwards, 1997 #234; Gehl, 1986 #275; Guarino, 1995 #318; Hill, 1989 #368; Kinlaw, 1991 #458; Luijpen, 1973 #497; Magnus, 1995 #507; Miller, 1973 #546; Mood, 1965 #551; Newport, 1985 #569; Nuechterlien, 1995 #595; Ott, 1971 #606; Rorty, 1993 #693; Ruf, 1989 #698; Saunders, 1976 #705; Schner, 1980 #713; Smith, 1986 #742; Spagnolo, 1975 #750; Thiselton, 1970 #776; Thiselton, 1980 #778; Thiselton, 1992 #775; Trundle, 1995 #795; Trundle, 1995 #797; Trundle, 1996 #796; Waismann, 1979 #817; Walsh, 1985 #820; West, 1979 #826; Witherspoon, 1996 #854; Xirau, 1986 #862]

Hermeneutics

[Apel, 1966 #17; Casper, 1976 #128; Embree, 1991 #239; Fahrenbach, 1971 #247; Fiorenza, 1987 #257; Gill, 1988 #281; Grassi, 1976 #309; Habermas, 1986 #324; Hustwit, 1980 #405; McFarlane, 1996 #530; Macquarrie, 1967 #500; Raschke, 1978 #675; Stines, 1980 #758; Thiselton, 1970 #776; Thiselton, 1992 #775; Wabel, 1998 #815; Williams, 1988 #840; Yin, 1992 #864]

Hick, John

[D'Costa, 1985 #205; Keeling, 1977 #437; Perrett, 1981 #622; Romerales, 1992 #692]

Hinduism

[Alper, 1989 #9; Bhat, 1996 #65; Chakrabarti, 1988 #132]

Holmer, Paul

[Henderson, 1979 #354; Jones, 1971 #425; Ommen, 1980 #605; Rollefson, 1994 #691; Sherry, 1974 #729; Stewart, 1991 #757; Thistlethwaite, 1985 #779]

Homosexuality

[Bartley, 1992 #42; Boero-Vargas, 1998 #71; Rudebush, 1979 #696]

Humanism

[Cox, 1980 #183; Reiser, 1969 #681]

Hume, David

[Churchill, 1995 #145; Dilman, 1981 #216; Edwards, 1972 #235; Richards, 1978 #684; Richmond, 1970 #686; Sellars, 1969 #721]

Husserl, Edmund

[McFarlane, 1996 #530; Saunders, 1976 #705; Son, 1978 #747; Waismann, 1979 #817]

Immortality

[Anderson, 1972 #13; Edwards, 1972 #235; Garceau, 1975 #267; Phillips, 1970 #629; Phillips, 1996 #630; Purtill, 1975 #668;

Spieler, 1975-76 #752; Thornton, 1993 #785; Whittaker, 1983 #837]

Incarnation

[Brown, 1986 #91; Cook, 1987 #168; Surin, 1986 #762]

Inerrancy

[Geisler, 1977 #276; Geisler, 1978 #277]

Infallibility

[Cooke, 1975 #173]

Inter-religious dialogue

[D'Costa, 1985 #205; Jespers, 1998 #418]

James, William

[Baum, 1980 #46; Harvey, 1971 #345; Inbody, 1994 #408; Lujan-Martinez, 1998 #498; McDermott, 1970 #528; Tarbox, 1992 #768; Tarbox, 1994 #766]

Jaspers, Karl

[Nystrand, 1984 #597; Schweidler, 1993 #715]

Jesus Christ

[Arens, 1985 #22; Devenish, 1983 #209; Grassi, 1976 #309; Gruenler, 1981 #315]

Joyce, James

[Bourbon, 1996 #72]

Judaism

[Bar-Elli, 1993 #37; Chatterjee, 1990 #138; Chatterjee, 1992 #137; Cordua, 1997 #176; Drob, 1988 #228; Hill, 1987 #369; Lerner, 1994 #486; Nevo, 1987 #567; Nystrand, 1986 #596; Polish, 1977 #650]

Justification of Religion, see: Rational justification of religion

Kafka, Franz

[Bramann, 1975 #79; Bramann, 1975 #80; Fleischacker, 1982 #259]

Kant, Immanuel

[Burkhardt, 1983 #106; Chakrabarti, 1988 #132; Cheng, 1981 #139; Clegg, 1979 #160; Edwards, 1972 #235; Farrelly, 1973 #249; Ferber, 1986 #251; Geisler, 1977 #276; Gill, 1969 #290; Hampe, 1992 #337; Hargrove, 1986 #340; Hull, 1994 #401; Laura, 1973 #477; Lear, 1984 #481; Liverziani, 1971 #492; Loades, 1981 #493; Miller, 1973 #546; Nielsen, 1976 #576; Paltrinieri, 1991 #610; Sellars, 1969 #721; Son, 1978 #747; Waismann, 1979 #817; Young, 1984 #867]

Kaufman, Gordon

[Irwin, 1995 #413; Tarbox, 1993 #767]

Kerr, Fergus

[Churchill, 1992 #144; Larrimore, 1991 #472; Murphy, 1992 #561; Schweizer-Bjelic, 1990 #716]

Language game

Language philosophy

Language, religious

1973 #496; Macquarrie, 1967 #500; Martin, 1966 #520; Martin, 1972 #512; Martin, 1978 #514; Martin, 1979 #515; Martin, 1987 #516; Martinich, 1976 #522; McNulty, 1975 #539; Moen, 1979 #547; Mojtabai, 1967 #548; Mondin, 1993 #550; Morse, 1982 #558; Muyskens, 1974 #563; Nicholson, 1996 #570; Niedballa, 1993 #572; Nielsen, 1973 #577; Nielsen, 1975-1976 #585; Nielsen, 1982 #589; Nielsen, 1984 #582; Nielsen, 1986 #583; Norris, 1993 #593; Northrop, 1962 #594; O'Hear, 1978 #601; O'Hear, 1978 #602; O'Keeffe, 1980 #603; Parret, 1983 #612; Patterson, 1991 #615; Pence, 1974 #618; Phillips, 1970 #639; Phillips, 1989 #645; Portmann, 1986 #653; Poulain, 1970 #656; Power, 1978 #659; Putnam, 1991 #669; Raschke, 1974 #674; Raschke, 1978 #675; Raschke, 1978 #676; Reese, 1978 #680; Reiser, 1969 #681; Robinson, 1976 #690; Sherry, 1974 #729; Sherry, 1977 #730; Stagaman, 1977 #753; Tarbox, 1993 #767; Thistlethwaite, 1985 #779; van Buren, 1972 #801; Vanhoozer, 1986 #805; Vincent, 1985 #810; Wenderoth, 1982 #825; White, 1982 #831; Whittaker, 1974 #834; Wilson, 1973 #842; Zeis, 1976 #871]

Language, theory of

[Ayers, 1976 #28; Bahnsen, 1976 #29; Baldini, 1993 #30; Bell, 1968 #60; Bell, 1974 #57; Bell, 1995 #58; Blackstone, 1963 #68; Bourbon, 1996 #72; Burnyeat, 1999 #107; Casper, 1977 #126; Churchill, 1994 #153; Cox, 1975 #180; Eastmen, 1969 #231; Embree, 1991 #239; Erling, 1984 #243; Gehl, 1986 #275; Henry, 1967 #356; Rorty, 1993 #693; Sarot, 1993 #703; Waismann, 1965 #818]

*Lectures and Conversations in Aesthetics, Psychology and Religious Belief*

[Engel, 1969 #241; Grennan, 1976 #311; Puelles, 1993 #666; Radford, 1975 #672; Shalom, 1967 #723]

Marx, Karl

[Glebe-Moller, 1978 #295; Hubík, 1984 #385]

Mathematics

[Henry, 1967 #356; Henry, 1976 #355; Hull, 1994 #401; Jager, 1972 #415; Petri, 1984 #625]

Meaning is use

[Ayers, 1976 #28; Bassols, 1989 #43; O'Keeffe, 1980 #603]

Mennonites

[Guth, 1986 #322]

Metaphysics

[Altmann, 1987 #10; Bar-Elli, 1993 #37; Barrett, 1991 #40; Baum, 1992 #48; Cavell, 1996 #130; Chapman, 1989 #134; Churchill, 1983 #150; Clarke, 1967 #158; Clegg, 1994 #161; Cook, 1994 #172; Coughlan, 1986 #178; Coughlan, 1987 #177; Cox, 1975 #180; Daly, 1956 #194; Dilman, 1975 #218; Dipre, 1968 #219; Garver, 1971 #270; Geisler, 1978 #277; Genova, 1970 #278; Glidden, 1996 #299; Grim, 1988 #314; Haller, 1989 #330; Hampe, 1992 #337; Harvey, 1971 #345; Holmes, 1969 #381; Jager, 1972 #415; Jones, 1975 #427; Keller, 1981 #444; Liverziani, 1971 #492; Luijpen, 1973 #497; MacIntyre, 1970 #499; Maesschalck, 1990 #503; Martin, 1981 #519; Martin, 1997 #513; McGuinness, 1966 #533; Nebreda, 1994 #564; Nielsen, 1972 #574; Pradhan, 1993 #661; Reiser, 1969 #681; Richmond, 1970 #686; Romerales, 1992 #692; Ryder, 1982 #700; Sellars, 1969 #721; Sherry, 1972 #728; Shields, 1997 #734; Smith, 1986 #742; Spagnolo, 1975 #750; Trundle, 1995 #797; van Buren, 1972 #801; Wahlström, 1986 #816; Westphal, 1995 #829; Whittaker, 1983 #837; Young, 1986 #870]

Methodology

[Bochenski, 1984 #69; Brümmer, 1993 #97; Carlson, 1982 #123; Clayton, 1974 #159; Creegan, 1989 #187; Fairley, 1991 #248; Genova, 1970 #278; Goff, 1970 #300; Hill, 1989 #368; Holmes, 1969 #381; Hurley, 1985 #402; Incandela, 1985 #409; Jasper, 1985 #417; Kelsey, 1980 #447; Kerr, 1991 #451; Kerr, 1992 #450; Kerr, 1997 #453; Munz, 1997 #560; Nicholson, 1996 #570; Nielsen, 1984 #582; Ommen, 1980 #605; Patterson, 1992 #614; Peterson, 1980 #624; Phillips, 1993 #642; Pierre, 1994 #646; Power, 1976 #660; Scharfstein, 1976 #709; Thomas, 1999 #781; Visvader, 1978 #811]

Miracle

[Garceau, 1975 #267; Grafrath, 1997 #306; Hustwit, 1980 #405; Joubert, 1986 #428; McKnight, 1984 #535; Moore, 1988 #552; Palmer, 1995 #609; Rowe, 1989 #695]

Moore, G. E.

[Armengaud, 1983 #23; Britton, 1962 #88; Cell, 1978 #131; Charlesworth, 1970 #135; Gill, 1974 #287; Hartnack, 1981 #343; Jones, 1975 #427; Lazerowitz, 1976 #480; Magee, 1971 #504; Moran, 1997 #556; Shields, 1987 #733; Wallace, 1984 #819]

Murdoch, Iris

[Gurrey, 1990 #321]

Mysticism

[Almond, 1979 #6; Antiseri, 1973 #16; Arcenas, 1974 #18; Arnswald, 1998 #26; Barrett, 1992 #39; Baum, 1980 #46; Boero, 1994 #70; Breton, 1975 #87; Burr, 1976 #108; Burrows, 1993 #111; Canfield, 1975 #119; Caraboolad, 1976 #121; **Chapman,**

1989 #134; Churchill, 1994 #152; Cox, 1976 #182; Cox, 1979 #181; Gehl, 1986 #275; Grabner-Haider, 1975 #304; Graham, 1984 #307; Greisch, 1991 #310; Grillo, 1997 #313; Hellerer, 1984 #351; Hoffman, 1960 #372; Horne, 1976 #383; Hudson, 1979 #386; John, 1988 #420; Kerr, 1998 #452; Lujan-Martinez, 1998 #498; McCabe, 1992 #525; McDermott, 1970 #528; McGuinness, 1966 #533; McHale, 1979 #534; Murphy, 1995 #562; Nevo, 1987 #567; Nieli, 1987 #573; Northrop, 1962 #594; Popov, 1997 #651; Portmann, 1986 #654; Poulain, 1970 #656; Rowe, 1989 #695; Smith-Eivemark, 1996 #746; Sontag, 1995 #748; Spaemann, 1973 #749; Todisco, 1991 #788; Tominaga, 1982 #789; Verbin, 1996 #808; Weeks, 1993 #822; Xirau, 1982 #863; York, 1997 #866; Zemach, 1964 #872]

Myth

[Baltazar, 1981 #32; Bouveresse, 1991 #74; Hurley, 1995 #403; Macquarrie, 1967 #500; Nielsen, 1976 #576; Thiselton, 1981 #773; Vergote, 1969 #809]

Nagarjuna

[Cheng, 1981 #139; Katz, 1977 #434; McLean, 1986 #538; Schroeder, 1996 #714]

Natural theology

[Brümmer, 1994 #98; Clarke, 1967 #158; Richmond, 1970 #686]

Negative theology

[Baum, 1980 #46; Baum, 1982 #44; Baum, 1992 #48; Berenson, 1984 #64; Burrows, 1993 #111]

Neo-Orthodoxy

[Cheng, 1982 #140; Clayton, 1974 #159; Madden, 1967 #501]

Newman, John Henry

[McCarthy, 1982 #526]

Nielsen, Kai

[Diamond, 1986 #214; Garceau, 1975 #267; Huang, 1995 #384; Hudson, 1968 #390; Incandela, 1985 #409; Yong, 1995 #865]

Nietzsche, Friedrich

[Craft, 1984 #184]

Nihilism

[Edwards, 1997 #234; King-Farlow, 1984 #457; Kinlaw, 1991 #458]

*Notebooks, 1914-1916*

[Pradhan, 1993 #661; Sayre, 1981 #707; Sievert, 1994 #736; Vargas, 1989 #806]

Nygren

[Erling, 1984 #243; Geisler, 1978 #277; Hall, 1979 #329]

O'Hara, Scarlet

[Davies,1982 #199]

Omnipotence

[Clarke, 1967 #158]

Omniscience

[Clarke, 1967 #158]

*On Certainty*

[Gill, 1974 #287; High, 1981 #366; Langworthy, 1984 #471; Martin, 1984 #517; Robinson, 1976 #690; Shields, 1997 #734; Wallace, 1984 #819]

Ontotheology

[Edwards, 1989 #232; Hill, 1989 #368; Ruf, 1989 #698; Smith, 1986 #742]

Ordinary Language

[Garner, 1977 #268; Keller, 1981 #444; Martin, 1966 #520; Nieli, 1987 #573; Parret, 1983 #612; Short, 1992 #735; Smith, 1979 #745]

Pantheism

[Garver, 1971 #270]

Paradox

[Ferreira, 1994 #253; Herbert, 1979 #358; Lippitt, 1998 #491; Visvader, 1978 #811; Wisdom, 1965 #852]

Pascal, Blaise

[Long, 1969 #495; Moran, 1997 #556; Morot-Sir, 1974 #557]

Peirce, Charles Sanders

[Hull, 1994 #401; Mullin, 1961 #559; Reiser, 1969 #681; Upper, 1992 #800]

Percy, Walker

[Churchill, 1984 #146]

Phenomenology

[Gill, 1990 #291; Gruenler, 1981 #315; Hallett, 1991 #332; Henry, 1967 #356; Holmes, 1969 #381; Jones, 1975 #427; Newport, 1985 #569]

Phillips, D. Z.

[Barrie, 1980 #41; Bildhauer, 1972 #66; Burhenn, 1974 #102; Clack, 1995 #155; Cook, 1988 #171; D'Costa, 1985 #205; Dilley, 1976 #215; Ferreira, 1995 #254; Fitzpatrick, 1978 #258; Grennan, 1976 #311; Gutting, 1982 #323; Haikola, 1976 #327; Henderson, 1979 #354; Henderson, 1985 #353; Huang, 1995 #384; Incandela, 1985 #409; Kasachkoff, 1970 #433; Kellenberger, 1979 #440; Klinefelter, 1974 #460; Kuitert, 1981 #464; Lerner, 1994 #486; O'Keeffe, 1980 #603; Ommen, 1980 #605; Purtill, 1975 #668; Ray, 1990 #677; Richards, 1978 #685; Shepherd, 1976 #726; Sherry, 1972 #731; Yong, 1995 #865]

*Philosophical Investigations*

[Bourbon, 1996 #72; Brenner, 1999 #84; Goff, 1962 #301; Goff, 1970 #300; High, 1967 #363; Stashwick, 1983 #756; Wienpahl, 1979 #839]

Philosophical theology

[Burrell, 1970 #110; Coulson, 1958 #179; Davie, 1973 #198; Downey, 1983 #224; Gill, 1975 #288; Hill, 1987 #369; Inbody, 1994 #408; Insole, 1998 #412; Kaufman, 1999 #435; Keeling, 1977 #437; Larrimore, 1991 #472; McDonald, 1986 #529; Møller, 1968 #549; Murphy, 1992 #561; Ott, 1971 #606; Phillips, 1993 #642; Rollefson, 1994 #691; Wilson, 1973 #842]

Philosophy of language, see: language philosophy

Philosophy of religion

[Carlson, 1982 #123; Cathey, 1989 #129; Churchill, 1977 #147; Churchill, 1995 #145; Cleobury, 1970 #162; Coughlan, 1986 #178; Coughlan, 1987 #177; Cox, 1976 #182; Creegan, 1987 #186; Crunkleton, 1984 #191; Davis, 1984 #204; DeAngelis, 1994 #208; Diamond, 1986 #214; Dilman, 1975 #217; Dilman, 1975 #218; Edwards, 1972 #235; Fitzpatrick, 1978 #258; Fleming, 1988 #261; Foster, 1995 #262; Garceau, 1975 #267; Gill, 1982 #285; Gill, 1990 #291; Glebe-Moller, 1969 #298; Graf, 1984 #305; Greisch, 1991 #310; Grim, 1988 #314; Haden, 1991 #325; High, 1986 #365; High, 1990 #367; Holland, 1990 #374; Hubík, 1984 #385; Hudson, 1974 #391; Hudson, 1977 #395; Incandela, 1985 #409; Insole, 1998 #412; Johnson, 1991 #421; Kaufman, 1999 #435; Kellenberger, 1990 #443; Klinefelter, 1974 #460; Kurten, 1987 #466; Laura, 1972 #478; Leinfellner, 1978 #484; Martin, 1966 #520; Mattingly, 1995 #523; McKnight, 1984 #535; Moore, 1998 #553; Newport, 1985 #569; Nielsen, 1982 #581; Nystrand, 1984 #597; Oakes, 1992 #598; Phillips, 1991 #636; Pierre, 1994 #646; Portmann, 1986 #653; Punzo, 1982 #667; Richards, 1978 #685; Roberts, 1979 #687; Romerales, 1992 #692; Rowe, 1989 #695; Satris, 1978 #704; Sedmak, 1996 #719; Shepherd, 1974 #727; Stewart, 1991 #757; Tabor, 1983 #765; Tornos, 1989 #792; Verbin, 1996 #808; Whittaker, 1978 #838; Wuchterl, 1981 #861; Wuchterl, 1984 #860; Xirau, 1986 #862]

Postmodernism

[Drewniak, 1993 #227; Lindbeck, 1984 #490; Magnus, 1995 #507; Miller, 1986 #545; Nebreda, 1994 #564; Scott, 1991 #718; Sedmak, 1996 #719; Thiselton, 1995 #772; Työrinoja, 1997 #799]

Practice, religious

[Canfield, 1975 #119; Kelsey, 1980 #447; Phillips, 1995 #633]

Pragmatism

[Bahnsen, 1976 #29; Fiorenza, 1987 #257; Tarbox, 1994 #766]

Prayer

[Bassols, 1989 #43; Bell, 1986 #56; Henderson, 1985 #353; Hudson, 1973 #394; Kasachkoff, 1970 #433; Palma, 1988 #608; Phillips, 1965 #628; Saliers, 1980 #702]

Preaching

[Holmer, 1971 #377; Johnston, 1994 #423; Jones, 1971 #425; Krieg, 1997 #462; Peterson, 1980 #624]

Predestination

[Barrett, 1991 #40; Westergaard, 1998 #828; Whittaker, 1981 #836; Young, 1978 #869]

Private language

[Ayer, 1985 #27; Downing, 1972 #225; Gurrey, 1990 #321; Jacquette, 1996 #414; Parret, 1983 #612; Perrett, 1981 #622; Sedmak, 1996 #719; Spieler, 1975-76 #752; Topping, 1993 #791; Työrinoja, 1984 #798]

Realism

[Beards, 1995 #49; Ferreira, 1995 #254; Helme, 1981 #352; Kerr, 1997 #455; Miller, 1995 #543; Sellars, 1969 #721; Spagnolo, 1975 #750]

Reformation

[Bretall, 1987 #86]

Relativity

[Bruce, 1988 #92; Hurley, 1985 #402; Johnstone, 1993 #424; McDonald, 1986 #529; Moen, 1979 #547; Placher, 1989 #648; Power, 1978 #659; Wahlström, 1986 #816; Winch, 1976 #845]

Religion, general

[Bambrough, 1989 #33; Baum, 1979 #45]

Religious belief, see: Belief, religious            .

Religious experience

[Gill, 1969 #290; Harvey, 1971 #345; Henderson, 1979 #354; Henderson, 1985 #353; Hoffman, 1960 #372; Hudson, 1974 #391; Hudson, 1981 #393; Hughes, 1968 #400; Magnanini, 1979 #506; Martin, 1981 #519; McDermott, 1970 #528; Needham, 1972 #565; Nielsen, 1973 #586; Proudfoot, 1976 #665; Reese, 1978 #680; Richmond, 1970 #686; Roberts, 1977 #689; Työrinoja, 1984 #798]

Religious language, see: Language, religious

Resurrection

[Devenish, 1983 #209; Surin, 1986 #762]

Revelation

[Disbrey, 1994 #220; Hustwit, 1985 #404; Leuze, 1984 #487; Raschke, 1978 #676; Trundle, 1995 #795; Vanhoozer, 1986 #805]

Rhees, Rush

[Dilman, 1981 #216; Lerner, 1994 #486; Phillips, 1989 #645]

Ricoeur, Paul

[Raschke, 1978 #675; Williams, 1988 #840]

Ritual

[Boero, 1994 #70; Churchill, 1992 #144; Churchill, 1995 #145; Clack, 1996 #156; Collins, 1996 #165; Davies,1983 #203; Erben, 1997 #242; Lerner, 1994 #486; Lillegard, 1984 #489; McGhee, 1996 #531; McGuinness, 1982 #532; Rhees, 1982 #683; Sachs, 1988 #701]

Rorty, Richard

[Anderson, 1990 #12; Caine, 1993 #113; Garner, 1985 #269; Glidden, 1996 #299; Incandela, 1985 #409; Magnus, 1995 #507; Thiselton, 1992 #775]

Royce, Josiah

[Glidden, 1996 #299; Paterno, 1995 #613]

Seeing-as

[Almond, 1979 #6; Churchill, 1998 #143; Heaney, 1979 #348; Hesse, 1969 #361; Raschke, 1978 #676; Reese, 1978 #680; Roberts, 1979 #687; Slater, 1980 #738]

Self

[Bell, 1978 #63; Caine, 1993 #113; Churchill, 1984 #146; Dilman, 1981 #216; Kinlaw, 1991 #458; Richards, 1978 #684; Thiselton, 1995 #772]

Semiotics

[Almeida, 1981 #5; Larson, 1978 #473]

Shaivism

[Alper, 1989 #9]

Showing/saying, see: Saying/showing

Silence

[Baldini, 1993 #30; Bindeman, 1978 #67; Dragona-Monachou, 1980 #226; Gehl, 1986 #275; Johnson, 1991 #421; Junker, 1996 #429; Long, 1969 #495; Scheier, 1991 #711]

Sin

[Shields, 1997 #734]

Skepticism

[Allen, 1972 #4; Armstrong, 1980 #25; Balmuth, 1984 #31; Barrett, 1994 #38; Bearn, 1984 #51; Bearn, 1993 #52; Browarzik,

1988 #90; Burke, 1978 #105; Churchill, 1984 #149; Churchill, 1987 #142; Churchland, 1987 #154; Clegg, 1979 #160; Cook, 1987 #168; Dilman, 1981 #216; Eisenstein, 1990 #236; Garner, 1977 #268; Gill, 1974 #287; Grant, 1995 #308; Gutting, 1982 #323; Haikola, 1977 #326; Hannay, 1990 #339; Harrison, 1988 #342; Harvey, 1971 #345; Heimbeck, 1969 #350; High, 1981 #366; High, 1986 #365; Kellenberger, 1983 #442; Kermode, 1990 #449; Lachel, 1974 #468; Martin, 1991 #521; Mattingly, 1995 #523; Needham, 1972 # 5 6 5 ; Nepomechie, 1993 #566; Nielsen, 1973 #586; Nielsen, 1986 #583; Nielsen, 1989 #580; O'Hear, 1978 #601; Olmsted, 1980 #604; Parret, 1983 #611; Penelhum, 1986 #620; Phillips, 1970 #644; Phillips, 1996 #630; Priestley, 1982 #663; Proudfoot, 1976 #665; Ray, 1990 #677; Shelley, 1995 #725; Tilghman, 1998 #786; Wallace, 1984 #819; Whittaker, 1974 #834; Whittaker, 1981 #836; Whittaker, 1988 #833; Witherspoon, 1996 #854]

Solipsism

[Churchill, 1983 #150; Davie, 1973 #198; Haller, 1989 #330; Huff, 1992 #399; Perrett, 1981 #622; Thornton, 1993 #785]

Soul

[Bourbon, 1996 #72; Gillett, 1985 #294; McGhee, 1996 #531; Phillips, 1996 #630;   Savigny, 1995 #706; Thiselton, 1973 #774; Whittaker, 1983 #837]

Spengler, Oswald

[DeAngelis, 1994 #208]

Spinoza, Babuch

[Garver, 1971 #270; Geisler, 1978 #277; Hampe, 1992 #337; Strickler, 1973 #759;   Winch, 1989 #847]

Tillich, Paul

[Cell, 1978 #131; Clayton, 1974 #159; Dilman, 1981 #216; Hall, 1963 #328; Hudson, 1974 #393; Kellner, 1985 #447; Macquarrie, 1967 #500; Madden, 1967 #501; Martin, 1978 #514; Miller, 1973 #546; Schmidt, 1985 #712]

Tolstoy, Leo

[Archer, 1985 #20; Baum, 1977 #47; Baum, 1980 #46; Hellerer, 1984 #351; Magnanini, 1979 #506; Puelles, 1993 #666; Thomas, 1997 #780; Thompson, 1994 #783]

*Tractatus Logico-Philosophicus*

[Abramson, 1987 #1; Arcenas, 1974 #18; Arnswald, 1998 #26; Baum, 1992 #48; Boutin, 1990 #73; Churchill, 1983 #150; Churchill, 1984 #146; Churchill, 1994 #152; Dragona-Monachou, 1980 #226; Elstein, 1991 #238; Ferber, 1986 #251; Hellerer, 1984 #351; Hess, 1989 #360; Hudson, 1981 #387; Jones, 1985 #426; Kroy, 1982 #463; Martin, 1988 #518; McGuinness, 1966 #533; McHale, 1979 #534; Møller, 1968 #549; Nevo, 1987 #567; O'Keefe, 1980 #603; Poulain, 1970 #656; Pradhan, 1993 #661; Puelles, 1993 #666; Shalom, 1967 #723; Shields, 1997 #734; Spiegelberg, 1979 #751; Thornton, 1993 #785; Vargas, 1989 #806; Verbin, 1996 #808; Whittaker, 1983 #837]

Tracy, David

[Caldwell, 1998 #114; Downey, 1983 #224; Downey, 1986 #223]

Tradition

[Disbrey, 1994 #220; Dov Lerner, 1995 #222]